A growing list of your author's
books are attached in the back of
this book for your inspection.

Paradox of Progress Unfolding 1

A Tale of Progress and
The Adventures They Create

Lloyd E. McIlveen

Order this book online at www.trafford.com
or email orders@trafford.com

Most Trafford titles are also available at major online book retailers.

Print information available on the last page.

ISBN: 978-1-4907-0530-9 (sc)
ISBN: 978-1-4907-0529-3 (e)

Library of Congress Control Number: 2013913723

Trafford rev. 12/03/2015

 www.trafford.com

North America & international
toll-free: 1 888 232 4444 (USA & Canada)
fax: 812 355 4082

This story of the future isn't "only" of future vision. It will be a meaningful and exciting adventure that could influence the lives of yourself, your children and their children into the future.

Our whole life's accomplishments are results of accumulated understanding and the security we build within ourselves. We gather this understanding from the past and maybe a little from future sources.

You may already have a fine understanding of humanity and if that's true, reading this story "all the way through" will be rewarding with an added perspective and insight that can be used as leverage for strengthening your present and future security here on Earth or anywhere else.

Contents

Author's Introduction

Progress and expanded population throughout the world is only beginning to show signs of insurmountable problems. As the centuries unfold, the situation is becoming technologically better because it is being somewhat controlled.

However, an invisible monster of unforeseen proportion lurks and progresses among the people of planet Earth without their realizing or even caring.

Intelligence from a distant future has relayed a lengthily message back to our present time warning us of an impending disaster that has been in the creative making for centuries. It can be much worse than climate change and it is created by mankind.

A very few centuries down the road, if not less, will reveal clearer signs of the inevitable and overdue paradox of progress.

One of mankind's most frightening nightmares will be unveiled in a realistic manner. The human societies of the world will be forced to compromise with decisions in a panic state that will separate and turn them against one another by virtue of their impending fate and lust for power and survival.

Mankind will be, technologically, close to mastering ongoing space age projects, but they will make a mistake, as usual, of only being concerned about the now and very close future and not enough about a further and distant future. Brace yourself for this one. Wonders won't cease!

Preface

Hello. My name is D. B. I438-GR0008. I am relating to you, through your author, from a space time continuum in your very distant future.

Science fiction jargon? Be patient. I am from a phase of time where my language is different than yours in your time. I am translating my thoughts, again through your author, into your present realm of thinking so you can understand what it is I have to tell you.

My time in space refers to my being in your time not as having traveled in reverse across the universe so fast I can "get caught up with you," but as having transformed the energy of me through an intelligence where, if explained to you in your time, may not be understood. So trust me and know all intelligence in the universe must mature and unfold in it's natural form as time passes.

Needless to say, many episodes of great magnitude have developed in your time of the two thousand millennium.

The story I will be revealing to you in the scripts ahead will be an approximation of what may happen with humanity in your future. It may influence your thinking on which kind of environment you might choose for your future. It may also shake you up enough to curl your toenails overnight.

This story is about mankind's progress. That could be a determining factor in defeating the survival of human civilization.

As you know, technology of your time has been astounding because it has accelerated so fast from the years of nineteen hundred to two thousand. It has gone far beyond that in the next three hundred years or so.

All activity in the universe first triggers an action. Then there is a reaction. What makes it do that? That's like asking why. Humanity needs a little more time for those answers.

All we really know now is you and I can influence that reaction in guiding our desired direction as humans on planet Earth or anywhere else. The story reveals this.

Belief of what is, is only equal to perception based on the past. A little delving into the future might improve that perception. That's why I'm here.

We of many hundreds of years ahead in time have evolved in our belief that transcending comprehensible information from the future to the past is our responsibility toward maintaining man/ space equilibrium.

We have had the advantage, at least in comparing our eras, of many lessons by these unique abilities to transcend this story to you.

Whether or not this story really happens in your future depends entirely on how your era of generations respond to the story.

I will be narrating this story of centuries ahead in time, beginning with the year twenty three forty, so stay with me in this meaningful and terrifying episode of human destiny and you will acquire the needed perception to make major decisions pertaining to the survival of mankind if you choose to do so.

Remember this: The story is not primarily about individuals. It is about humanity.

Terminology utilized
in centuries of the future

P. 8 & 9 Capsulecars: Small flight cars capable of moving in any direction by nuclear propulsion. They are pressurized for higher elevated flight.

P. 7 & 9 ESR (earth space regulators): An international capsulecar control agency.

P. 7 & 9 Ossoscan fibriolator: Personal telecommunicator.

P. 16 WOAC: World architectural controllers.

P. 26   WCR: World community of religion which deals with interrelated religious issues.

P. 46   IWC: Electrokenetic atmosviewers for constant audio/video.

P. 27   ORL: Ossoscan recording library. Accessible by ossoscan.

P. 27   Compulvisioners used with electrokenetic atmosviewers.

P. 28   EGA: Environmental guidance agency (world temperature).

P. 44 & 49   WRG: World renavator group. A mixed nation group of financial conglomerates helpful for all projects.

P. 27. 31 & 52   Photocard contract: Access to legal matters through ORL by everyone.

P. 51   Time estimating calculator: Measures gravity weight and loss.

P. 54 & 106   Electrode positrating encomagnet inducer ray for regulating out of atmosphere reactions.

P. 54   Whipstreakers: Nuclear controlled space vessels of various sizes.

P. 80   Weightless offsetters. Artificial gravity in space stations.

P. 46, 88 & 163   Spaceview screen: Distance magnifying focuser.

P. 46 & 163   Lazer designator: Sends messages
through space.

P. 121, 131, 133, 134, 135 & 138 Tricoal: Financial
conglomerate leading the space people.

P. 151   Comviewer: A tricky communication
detector.

P. 157   EMK: Central control in space stations.
Electrodynamic and kenetic frequency
modulator.

P. 46 & 163   Astrometric viewer: A long range viewer
to observe stations and the planet Mars. A
lazorscopic measuring sensor which assists
the atmosviewer.

Chapter 1

When overpopulation finally reaches a saturation point

The year is 2340. "Mom," says Arthur Flintstock's son Jack, "We don't have sports in school any more because there's no more room for it. Their using the room for classes. I can't even get into the pool any more because of so many kids."

Arthur is preparing to depart from home on a historic adventure that could change the coarse of humanity. He has a wife and four children who are all living under extreme pressure of stress and anxiety.

An obvious condition of overpopulation is facing all the people on planet Earth. It is approaching a squeezing stage with no relief.

Arthur has decided to form an alliance of people to solve the problem of overpopulation that has been progressively plaguing the world uncontrollably for over a century.

Prior to two thousand A.D., overpopulated areas of the world like Asia, India, Africa etc. were a creeping threat to the world especially when that problem began spreading throughout Europe and the Americas.

That condition remained somewhat contained in the twentieth century because of natural disasters including earthquakes, tornadoes, floods, disease, famine and war which killed many people.

Time passed later in that century and technology began to surge, new inventions flooded the market so fast mankind suffered complex sociological and industrial growing pains in adapting to rapid change.

Shortly after that, around the turn of the century, the people of the world began to manage their growth better and became more competitive for gaining life's needs.

Wars began to progressively diminish somewhat and food production increased through world competition and cooperation.

The following decades and centuries passed and mankind achieved what seemed like an unfolding of wonderful and rewarding accomplishments.

Through new technological innovations, man has conquered the earthquake and tornado problems by sending electro static gamma ray reducers into magnetic polarizers, thereby calming radical molecular tendencies.

Through world coops, man has also equalized and controlled the water supply and flooding by utilizing industrial energies through giant resignators vibrating atmospheric pressure in such a way that water is literally turned off and on to meet the peoples demands. More water and food has become available with a robustly expanding society. The world's deserts and open lands have filled in with buildings and people. More people have been eating, working, having children and there has been funds for health research and use which has almost eliminated physical disease.

The control of empires, as a result of wars, is no longer accepted in resolving disputes of power. Power is no longer perceived as a belief where mankind must be coerced or controlled by self-centered leaders who pose an omnipotent threat to others.

Money and credit is still used daily, but has been applied more resourcefully for the purpose of educating people on how to promote progress without hiring overpowering and radical leadership.

That power is fairly contained at this time. The people of the world have seen the results of sharing and agree that sharing is a power that has brought more rewards of progress to everyone.

That's the positive view. There is also another side to this phenomenon. While everyone is enjoying the fruit of the future in all aspects, those aspects are becoming unbearable in the sense there is simply too much of everything. There are no longer a few billion people, but has far surpassed that figure. There are no longer endless plains of real estate to expand and build on. Escaping to a desolate retreat is a commodity of past centuries. Burying and cremating the dead is now becoming a square footage problem. Farms no longer exist on flat land. That land has been filled in with housing, business and industry. All farms are now maintained in virticle high rise open buildings with sunlight control design.

Now people are beginning to view their expanding progress at the present as setting the pace for defeat in time. They are not quite clear on what reality they must face.

People are cooperative with one another because they know if they don't, they may have to experience a general panic that will disturb their present way of life.

Arthur's wife disagrees with his departure. She thinks something bad might happen to him and he may never come back. His children are too young to hypothesize. They just don't want him to go. Arthur knows something terrible could happen to all of them if he does nothing.

The decision is made. Arthur contacts a buddy of his named Ron West, who is ready and waiting to get started forming a group for their survival strategy.

Several months of discussion has occurred between twenty four people around the world. All of them have finally agreed to take the initiative and compile their efforts toward preventing chaos from overpopulation.

Mankind has been so smart in creating this massive population; let's see if they can resolve the problem.

They have decided to meet, all under the general direction of Arthur Flinstock. The meeting place will be at the recently formed government rally arena which is a modulized, flat and nonflamably inflated gas suspended platform like a giant balloon elevated one thousand feet above the surface of the ocean which is set up on quick notice and can support four million vehicles called capsulecars. They are small flying cars capable of moving in any direction, are driven by nuclear propulsion and are pressurized for higher elevation and faster flying. Their disposition is strictly regulated by an international space control agency called Earth Space Regulators (ESR) who set and enforces rules of respect, direction, detection and penalties.

Each one of the twenty four people have agreed to contact fifty people around the world. Those fifty people will, in turn, bring in fifty people etc., etc. like a pyramid program of the twentieth century.

Verbal communication is second to none in efficiency. Almost everyone has a small device called an ossoscan fibriolator that reaches anyone anywhere in the world by the use of a simple mathematical adjustment of which everyone is taught as they begin to learn language.

Arthur and Ron said goodbye to their families and are on their way to rendezvous with their first crusaders. They are both traveling in their own capsulecars so they can recruit others and guide them to the meeting pad.

There are no roads; only designators, which is a laser beam of light projected from one station to the next (stations are a type of crossway). There are no trucks or trains any more. All material goods and food are lifted and flown to their destinations by transloaders. These are flying vehicles which are ejected upward similar to a rocketship. They move up on an angle in a calculated path toward its destination; reaches a peak; then descends on an angle to land at a given spot.

The ESR provides right of way privileges for these ships and medical transportation. However, they are all equipped with a radar detection "bumper" which prevents accidents with other flying vehicles.

"Be careful on the designator today," says Arthur to Ron on the ossoscan. "I heard there will be more traffic out due to monthly traffic investigations (the traffic system is checked monthly by a large fleet of official vehicles for efficiency and cooperation. Citations are not issued. If people have a monthly monitored record of not maintaining harmony on the designator, a magnetic vacuum beam is applied to noncooperating vehicles, is towed off the designator and deactivated at the expense and inconvenience of the operator)."

"Let's call ESR and request shifting to a higher elevation where more speed on lengthy destinations is allowed." "Agreed," responds Ron. "This will take forever plowing through millions of people on "parents day."

Everyone is pretty cooperative with the system. They have learned from birth that cooperation creates compatibility and that's the way the system keeps working.

Arthur and Ron have traveled two hundred miles in just a few minutes and are moving toward their destinations to branch out in different directions.

They are now approaching the change off station. Arthur says, "See you after we drag four million people around the world to meet at the arena." "Right," says Ron. "We might need some luck. After all, these are just ordinary people we are dragging!"

A few hours have passed. Arthur and Ron have made contact with two million people and they are all forming a massive flock, like birds, in the sky. They are moving from all directions almost like drifting leaves being vacuumed into formation.

The sight is awesome. The flock casts a shadow over the population and buildings which, in turn, infests its massive display of progress back on the flock.

The capsulecars are now following a path of predetermined designator elevations.

The higher the massive flocks go, the more ESR they must comply with because of other space travelers ascending and descending.

Ron is anxious in his quest to be a leader. He means well and has a heart of gold, but he is also caught up in this vacuum of needs from an almost desperate society of too many people. He is a good technician and gets along pretty good with people, but his emotions are beginning to overwhelm him. He has the feeling this moving flock of cars are gaining momentum behind him. He's not a professional flier, just an energetic concerned citizen.

The result of this emotional influence is he really has too much responsibility and his objectives are not being kept in check. His portion of the flock is tending to slant semi parallel toward Arthur's flock while being filled in by new arrivals.

Arthur detects the breach of formation and calls Ron. "Your lead projection is off the designators and will result in my fleet's necessity to conform to your angle. That will throw us off in meeting our last ten adjoining fleets. I know it's difficult to see designators through these clouds, but you have to get back on track or we may collide and that's not my favorite maneuver right now," he says.

The new adjoining flocks are beginning to fill in and it's getting real tight.

Ron is trying hard to maneuver his flock back in line, but the new ones are coming in on track too fast.

Arthur is sweating it out and knows it's real risky to do it, but makes a decision to lead his flock off on an angle to compensate. The message is relayed on the ossoscan to the new cars coming in. Through Arthur's skill and efforts of very cooperative people, a miracle has happened and four million people are all on track now, but it's not on designated track.

The chances of arriving precisely on target are almost none now. They will have to rely on fair weather and better judgment.

Ron is embarrassed, but staying focused on leading his people. He is emotionally collected now and the whole flock of four million capsulecars are heading somewhat in the direction of the arena.

A few minutes reveal, off to the left, the giant international floating pad. A facility which permits political rallies only.

All cars are approaching the pad under manual control. Being off their coarse makes it more difficult for all to land according to expectations, so everyone is concentrating in a state of dismay.

The general rule of flock landing is for everyone to circle the landing spot and follow the one in front. Safety reasons require more time needed for landing than a flock of birds. Mass confusion and accidents are avoided with precautionary methods such as flying slowly.

Instead of coming in on a tight whip circle and because of being off course, they veered off into a much larger circle and finally all turned in for descending to the pad one by one.

Each capsulecar landing has displayed an unusually and rather exciting sight of skill and courage for this many nonmilitary participation.

Well, they have arrived with all their people and just like most of everything else on planet Earth, with no fatalities. This may just be part of the subject for discussion at the meeting.

Chapter 2

Gathering to face the oncoming disaster

Four million people and government officials are moving into their places. The politicians, who are the listeners, gather in the foreground and the people, who are the speakers, remain in their capsulecars. Everyone can hear and be heard by making an adjustment on their ossoscans.

Since Arthur was the initiator of this rally, the majority have agreed that he has the distinction of speaking first.

Arthur rotates his transparent topped capsulecar roof toward the back out of the way and elevates his seat so his body is half way out and clearly seen.

These capsulecars are very small, but they can pack a lot of them in to close quarters.

Arthur speaks to the crowd: "Our population has exploded to the point of becoming a threat to our existence. The nations of the whole world have been experiencing tremendous peacetime growth in food, homes, business and the most serious one of them all; our population."

"It seems almost everyone has agreed, up to recent decades, that growth in all areas has been healthy and has kept our families well supplied with almost everything we need."

"Well, this all has been great, but now it is time to take a realistic look at what is happening and will continue to happen and what prices we will have to pay for all this luxury and convenience."

"There is no land left to use for more expansion. The World Organization of Architectronic and Building Construction (WOABC) has determined, after an evaluation of high rise buildings over one hundred stories, not only the height of them, but the amount of them will create mass disasters when the coming earthquakes estimated mature. Every city has too many of them. They have penetrated and become part of the suburbs. Due to the use of the electromagnetic gamma ray reducers, the Earth's surface substance layers have been crumbling and creating a gas stream that is seeping out of the Earth from deep inside. This heat has been charged with our man-made earthquake treatments for nearly three hundred years and is being pulled out of the Earth by the static atmospheric vacuum that has been created as a result of tornado treatments."

"The results of all this earthly activity will inevitably create catastrophic earthquakes to say the least." Arthur hesitates a few seconds and says,

"So, how does all this fit into what to do about the population explosion? Keep listening and you will know."

"Looking forward to these disasters is unnerving and creates an ill sense of security. Actually experiencing them will not only be unfair to mankind because of not preventing them from happening, but the suffering of all mankind will be unimaginably and miserably intolerable, especially after experiencing the security of peace, serenity and luxury for centuries."

"From the human standpoint of view, anything that disturbs our way of life is considered bad, dangerous and must be stopped. This can no longer be our reasoning for existing. Planet Earth is normally a dangerous place to live and we are making it worse!"

"Actually, the whole universe is a dangerous place and we could probably make it worse too; given enough time."

"So, what we have to do is learn to accept natural disasters because apparently that's the way it was meant to be as long as we do our part in keeping it natural."

"Scientists have proven what we interpret as disasters is the way the universe has been functioning forever and here we are throwing a part of it off-key from its norm."

"I'd like now to let my friend and neighbor elaborate a little more on possibilities for solutions. Meet Ron West."

An agreement with massive handclapping is not in the best interests for this type of meeting because it is not meant to enhance anyone's glory and is retained quietly throughout the meeting.

Ron also stands in his capsulecar to speak. "My personal interest is to help make this world of ours somewhat tolerable for now and future generations. Some of us may have to go through some suffering at one time or another. What I don't want to see is all of us suffering constantly until we are all gone."

"The way I see it, our progress is beginning to reach maximum proportions toward an inevitable breach. Almost everytime we innovate something strategic to make it easier and/or better for us, we are creating a side effect that will sooner or later take its tole in injury and lives."

"What we need to do is flow along more with the ways of nature. What we need to do is support the ways of nature. Almost all of the world's ancient tribes knew about blending with nature and disasters weren't really a threat of extinction for the world."

"What we need to do now is not reverse our progress, but change our approach from thinking how well off we can be as individuals to realizing how well off the world can be by joining and supporting philosophy of nature and nature's function as it was meant to be."

"What we need to do is alert the people of the world to make some changes that will change this calamity of growth. The whole world is what caused these problems and it is the responsibility of the whole world to bring its people power together to work and solve the problems before it's too late."

"What we need to do is constitute world rules governed by the Institution of World Coop (IWC) which is a worldwide committee of representatives that helps form and support ideas for strategic use. They can limit the amount of humans born per family until such a time when we have reduced the population and adjusted to maintaining that limit."

"What we need to do is face our present destiny which is beginning to show signs of cracking. The very fact everything in every way is expanding gives rise to the possibility everything will either break down and/or explode from exceeding capacity."

"If we aren't willing to change and make sacrifices now, the progress will commence with staggering overpopulation and will become uncontrollable and we will all suffocate in our own progress just like any kind of triggering explosion. The only difference is the triggering may be a little slower and agonizing."

"If we wait, in a state of delusion thinking it will all resolve through further research, technology and new projects to compensate, we will be making a grave mistake. Whenever any project gets too large, many mistakes become eminent and subject to probability."

"An example is when I was leading over a million people toward this area, I thought we were on track. When I discovered we weren't, it was too late to change the direction for that many people. We arrived here safely, but dependent on luck and that must be reduced."

"We must not depend on confidence and luck any more. We must use our objective intelligence and resources to turn this dilemma around or face possible extinction."

The crowd on the giant pad is becoming more interested, excited and scared now and the urge to speak their views is becoming overwhelming.

Several people have raised their commsigns (lighted flags) indicating their desire to talk.

Ron has dismissed himself knowing now the momentum of chaos potentials has been revealed and all possibilities will probably be exposed.

The committee leader directs a laser pointer at a woman's commsign for permission to speak.

"This whole scenario sounds very negative. Are we supposed to make changes based on terrible things happening? I would rather make changes based on growing out of this situation of too many people by educating every person on how to manage more people and utilize the expansion concept through more and brighter minds. We could build fabulous underground, undersea and in the air cities. We could extract more natural resources from the Earth's internal supply. We could build more and bigger space stations. There are endless possibilities compared to reversing or slowing down our existing progress.

Several speakers have shared their thoughts and feelings pro, con and interim. The committee has been recording and documenting every word for evaluation when they return to their own lands.

The majority of the day has passed and everyone is weary and hungry, so the meeting is closed and the people have been notified all will be considered and brought to a vote through the voting system in a matter of days.

The capsulecars exit in the reverse direction, but in a slower manner than they landed. They are not flying in mass formation now like before. They are now moving in single line procedure. As they move out, they gain more speed so as to hasten the flock's exit.

More designators are turned on for this purpose with all these people racing home.

Two capsulecars brushed against each other which, in turn, caused a chain reaction of bumping. Six capsulecars were forced to descend to the pad and experience the inconvenience of an air accident. No one was killed and the rest of them have returned to their own areas of the world.

Out of four million people, that's not bad; or is it? That is a paradox of overpopulation. One goal mankind has been striving for in the past four hundred years has been to save lives. They have been successful in having to face the possibility of smothering out those lives through overpopulation.

The question has arisen many times lately as to whether the people will save lives as they push and shove each other around or whether they will break their trend of habits and deal with major change.

Chapter 3

The people are resisting to save Earth

There are many questions being presented by the people and analyzed for making decisions concerning survival of the people on Earth by the IWC.

One political party of the world wants birth control reform with heavy penalties for those who do not comply. The World Congregation of Religion (WCR) contends mass praying will solve the problem and still another party encourages education for volunteer suicide by anyone who is not participating in social reform.

The world's people have been living in a deceptive fantasy for several hundred years and now is having to pass through an all out state of hard hitting reality.

It's a very painful and confusing time requiring everyones attention. The job of voted representatives can only bounce back the ideas the people have presented to them because they are not allowed to make quick decisions for fast change.

They present the feedback to the people on world electrokenetic atmosviewers by the IWC which is a constant picture and sound just above the surface of the Earth. Everyone can see and hear outside or inside their compuvisioners or in their capsulecars. The data passes through a state of technical maturity that results in easier understanding for evaluation. The people then respond by returning than through the Ossoscan Recording Library (ORL).

The year is 2352. A few years have passed without much change. Arthur Flintstock is dedicated in follow up work that helps promote the cause. He and his companion Ron, who is also dedicated, are conducting a survey on their compuvisioners to help determine the progress.

It is critically important everyone has similar views on which method is used to solve this problem.

On the ossoscan, Ron tells Arthur, "I have contacted several million people around the world and have found, unfortunately, there are quite a mixture of opinions. Almost everyone wants to do something. They just want to do it in different ways."

"By the way," says Ron, "I checked with Environment Guidance Agency (EGA) concerning their long term world temperature averages. They said world temperature averages have increased fourteen percent in two hundred years."

"Yes," Arthur responds, "this has been happening for quite sometime now and appears to be adjacently relative to the population expansion. It must be too much creative energy activity and hot bodies! Increasing ambient temperatures are also affecting all living beings on Earth which makes this whole dilemma worse."

"I hate to say it," Ron says with dramatic emotion, "but maybe the world's people need a good scare to unite them for deciding what to do a little quicker."

Arthur replies, "That scare may have to appear in the form of a disaster in order to really bring them together. Human beings have always procrastinated in their habits before making critical decisions. I suggest we contact a few more groups, then transfer our findings to the IWC." The year is 2354. The people of the world have been tossing this overpopulation problem around for several years with still more focus on individual and family need than having the willingness to make sacrifices of change even with rising world temperatures from increasing progress.

The masses are growing a little faster now. The temperature is rising slowly and atmospheric pressure is beginning to show signs of lessening.

We see powder from the ground rising into the sky and not returning. This, theoretically, means Earth is losing its gravity.

Arthur and Ron have been alerted of this phenomenon and are taking the initiative to spread the word.

This powder rising is occurring around the world. If nothing is done about the population expansion soon, everything having any weight at all will rise beginning with the lightest weights such as tree leaves, feathers, pollens and yes, hair will stand on end!

Eventually, if not checked, everything and everybody will have to be strapped or weighted down. After that, whatever is holding the weights and straps will lift off and ascend into the sky. The sky will indeed be the new home of Earth's inhabitants if they have taken the time to learn how to live there.

Arthur and Ron again rounds up people for a meeting at the arena. This time, nine million people will be attending for more influence on faster than normal action. Because of the limited pad space, two separate meetings will be held.

This time, though, there are many casualties taking place because of the rising powders polluting the weakest of the capsulecars' motivators and just too many nervous vehicle operators.

However, the majority of the first batch have landed and the remainders are hovering overhead to remain in a somewhat stationary position.

Throughout the two sessions, more people expressed not only their views, but their fears almost to the point of panic. Their nerves and vehicles are breaking down and they are also scared their system of communicating and promoting will break down.

They are aware if that happens, it may be indeed, too late to make changes for reversing this dilemma.

Just as always, politics takes its course and time. With the journey completed again, the feed back process continues through efforts of the IWC and ORL.

The year is 2375. Technological progress is still scouring and more techniques are developing and directly offsetting the gravitational weakening. The problem is, it takes more energy to crystallize the atoms needed in rearranging the atmosphere's molecular structure for cooling off purposes. By virture of their using too much energy around the world, they are robbing that crystallization process. As time passes, they are defeating their purpose.

The world's people are so frantically attempting to solve the immediate problem of losing all their material accumulations to space, they appear psychologically incapable of dealing with long term preparation to change mankinds course of action for survival.

Arthur, Ron and all the people of the world who really want to make changes are working harder than ever with meetings and seminars to alert and teach the people how to understand and cope with the changes which are occurring.

The year is 2390. Arthur and Ron are well over a hundred now and beginning to slow down. They have helped make progress only in slowing down the inevitable. Their children have also joined in on the crusade of survival, but they too have been magnetized into the fast pace of mankind's progress and have found it difficult to do much about the dilemma other than invent ways and means of offsetting the forces confronting them daily.

The majority of the people seem to be "stuck" in a quagmire of day to day living and promoting their own activities.

Not enough of the world's people are getting serious about making changes. The result, so far, is where world legislatures are unable to initiate programs of major change.

The people of the world will no longer allow dominant governmental rule. They will no longer allow dictators or communal type rule.

Up to now, the best system of world regulation is securely engaged. The people and the legislators exchange their views repeatedly until the people finally accept what they think will work for the long run. After that, rules and laws are established.

The present state of dilemma is not because they can't make rules and laws and it isn't just because control has been lost by runaway momentum. It is because the people do not adhere to the rules and laws they have made that could prevent the dilemma. They are dragging along with the present progress of new innovations while lagging behind the new rules and laws.

Chapter 4

The threat of extinction brings in the conglomerates

The year is 2418. The population expansion continues. It is in a constant state of being checked and somewhat controlled because of the relentless efforts of crusaders like Arthur Flintstock, Ron West, their families and all the world's people they have been in contact with, but the material growth to offset disaster is still on the rise.

The people just don't seem to get the reality they have to stop, use discipline and undergo sacrifices in a larger magnitude of proportion than a hundred years or so ago.

Human progress now is not just greed of material possessions. It is greed of possessing their families and loved ones who are actually crushing themselves, as time passes, through overpopulation. This human progress is akin to a giant creature wrapped around the world eating first, on it's own tail, then on the rest of its own body.

As time passes, in this relentless momentum of defeat through growth, the lakes and seas of the world are slowly nebulizing upward into the sky along with the reoccurrence of land powder and now sand. The compensators can no longer retain the powder and water from lifting.

Again, mankind thinks they can get control over these man created conditions by using the heat scource of the condition with thousands of large jet turned turbine vacuum spreaders utilizing the very water it is attacking to solidify the ascending substances.

This process is working, for now, keeping millions of people busy supporting industry and their growing families.

The stance where containing earthly matter for reduction to heavier solids seemed logical at the time in a fit of panic, but the dilemma does not cease.

Everything is still growing in an over worked and weary society of the world. They are now beginning to realize they have worked hard only to defeat their cause which has been to keep the population alive and busy.

The year is 2420. Every time mankind invents something to compensate, it works for awhile, then it is defeated by natural forces.

Super progress and the gravity weakening is causing the needle on the health and stability machine to move over the peak and downward.

The result is the world's financial powers are pooling their resources with the idea of saving planet Earth. They saw this coming and have been using robots and reeducating and exploiting world trades people for building massive space stations out in space.

Their intensions are to convince world governments the best method of curing the problem of overpopulation is to continue building space stations and exploit planet Mars for inhabitation as soon as possible.

The "deal" is these conglomerates will have more influence over the people from that point forward.

The word gets around like wild fire and the majority wants to do it.

Arthur Flintstock is very old and decrepit now, but still sees how humanity has defeated themselves and advises his off springs to resist the offer and continue with some of the original rational plans to calm the Earth down.

Arthur is making a presentation to a crowd of thousands. He says, "It will, of course, be much more difficult to handle in this late stage, as I said many years ago, but the alternative of leaving planet Earth and being dominated by a space controlled conglomerate with possibilities to at least "live" as compared to remaining on Earth with its inevitabilities appear much more attractive. Methods of returning to Earth later may be resumed, so goes the talk."

Arthur adds a line from a song which came out of world war two over four hundred years ago that says "we did it before and we can do it again."

Arthur's kids are no longer very young either, but they are more philosophical now than they used to be and there is much more at stake, so they are participating more on the movement to change. They have accepted the challenge and are spreading the word "stay and accept your fate or leave and become subjects of power."

Mankind almost always thinks they are doing the right thing. Reality has it they could be destroying themselves.

The people have decided flocks of capsulecars are too dangerous and have outlawed them.

The system of established safety priorities is a two century ingrained rule and no one is willing to break it. Saving lives is a way of life. They believe the less flocks in the air, the less fatalities there will be. Their security is based on saving lives which eventually becomes a paradox of progress.

The ossoscan, with the proper adjustments, is about the only way of spreading the word of alternatives beside relaying it from one person to the next which is fairly easy since there are so many people so close together. Even the overuse of ossoscan is creating more heat that is weakening gravitational pull.

The oceans are bubbling slowly upward again along with the powder and the lightweight substances. The people of the world must do something fast or they won't have a chance to lift off in a spaceship to a space station; if that's what they decide.

When gravity lessons, all life and substance will begin lifting off the planet and won't return unless progress is reversed. They will begin to perish as soon as they lift off the ground without pressurized suits and supplies. There are some who are preparing for that inevitability, but even that has its limits.

The rate of accelerated progress is affecting Earth's atmosphere at present. Does the gravity loss indicate the Earth is crumbling apart and will end up a spiraling array of asteroids throughout our solar system?

Once mankind has left the Earth, however they do it, the equilibrium forces should resume to their destined courses and all will become normal again, in time, on planet Earth. This isn't the same as the climate change problem of the twenty first century which was technologically contained just in time in those days.

Prior to the making of the calendar and even up to the discovery of oil, humans weren't a destructive threat to themselves and to the Earth they lived on.

Even if all the people do evacuate Earth and relieve it of its burden, the existence of just one couple of both gender could start a repeat performance in the growth of mankind and their progress.

The amount of people on the Earth is staggering. They have been programmed to flow along like inertia with the present trends. They know they have to make changes like reducing procreation. Unfortunately, their beliefs are not only to expand their families, but to enjoy the preliminary activity.

Now, with the possible threat of extinction, they are upset, insecure and very emotional. Many have increased procreation activity with the deception of "everything will work out okay."

Arthur's oldest daughter Luanna is the most dynamic of all four of his children. The others help, but she is a born leader with unending determination.

She is constantly on the ossoscan recruiting people to spread the word to negotiate with the conglomerates.

Her belief is, along with millions of others where, at present, the people and the world are on a nonreversible course of elimination at present.

"It has gotten to the point of being too late," Luanna stresses on a wide broadcast. "My father told everyone several years ago waiting too long to change would make it too late to change. He was right. The only thing we can do now is attempt to save our hides by going to the space stations. There are enough of them being built by humans and robots from here to planet Mars."

"Planet Mars will be livable in a few years at the present rate of transformation. If we move now, we can help speed it up. Progress isn't nearly as great on the space stations at present, but we can help it."

"Besides," Luanne continues, "after the Earth has settled back to its normal state in a few years, many of us will be returning and hopefully, will be the ones who will promote living on our wonderful land in a more compatible manner with nature. Then the present disasters won't happen again, at least not in the foreseeable future."

"Meanwhile, it is crucial for us, the average of the population who have power in masses, to let our adversaries know we will be cooperative with them, but not become their slaves in this move to inhabit, work and developed a space living culture. They must be made aware we all have to want to work together to make this effort successful."

Shortly after, groups of a million people from around the world are gathering in designated areas for a communication with the world financial conglomerates.

These conglomerates are a smoothly run group of mixed nations, gender and age. They have retained a dependable reputation with sufficient resources called the World Renavator Group (WRG). Their function has been to save and promote weakened projects into successful ventures. They have a readiness availability that is second to none. Their organization has been built on the presumption whoever is there with the best, most and fastest will get the job and they have been constant in maintaining that posture.

WRG echelon officers are Eleasa McKonkey, Director. Anastas Muraste, Co Director of Natural Resource Excavations USA. Chum Kong, owner Physics Lab Asia. Ricardo Basade, President of Herbological Sources South America and Rudolph Boschev, President of European Siberian Bank, Europrussia.

Corporations are no longer a favorite for business protection. They are only an option. Asset protection becomes equal to their rate of progress which is not difficult to accomplish with the needs of so many people available. Business law is no longer regulated by a judicial system spending money on misjudging, correcting, changing and penelizing people in business.

The world business community acts constantly on enhancing and improving trade relationships with all people worldwide. Business disputes are solved before they happen with developed and cooperative mentality.

The world's society of people are far from perfect though. They are still humans who are exercising their finely tuned and sophisticated abilities to continue a sped up pace in their relentless quest to expand.

Communication with the WRG and IWC will commence through the technical assistance of Electro Kinetic Atmosviewers, a worldwide communication system that allows almost everyone wherever they are to view and hear a broadcast.

Eleasa McKonkey and her associates have been preparing for this immense communication and all of the WRG have arrived early as they usually do.

The place is a small floating island in a fairly calm area of the Pacific Ocean. Even though the water is squirting and bubbling upward from the diminishing gravity, this island is protected by a sealed bubble over the inhabited area. It is clearer here for world satellite reception to millions of people who will be viewing at their prospective meeting places around the world.

Chapter 5

Decisions to be partners or slaves

The year is 2424. Preparation for this meeting has been comparatively slow to their progress in general because they have been pooling so many ideas concerning a resolution.

The people of the world are ready to negotiate and decide, wherever it may go. They are all frightened and will do almost anything. These negotiations seem the only escape from dooms day at present.

Everyone will see and hear the speakers around the entire world. Bringing masses of people together like this for reasons of survival is creating a profound effect of joint efforts. The viewers are trembling with excitement and fear.

Chum Kong gives a general description of WRG's offer to the people: "Time is running short. The Earth's surface is lifting. Soon, we and everything else will be off the Earth and in to orbit and we will have no control over it. It will last until the Earth balances with time."

"We all have the opportunity to escape that destiny, but we must do it now. You can see the small particals on land and the water on oceans and lakes rising. We, of the WRG have the facilities, equipment and supplies to save mankind, animals and smaller forms of life which are important to the function of a living being planet. How to do this will be explained by my colleague from WRG Eleasa McKonkey."

Mrs. McKonkey says, "Our plan will be the simplest and the most effective way to survive at this time. We will direct you and you will follow our directions."

"Our moving into space has its benefits. The immediate reason is to survive this coming dilemma!

Then we will continue to promote the expansion of a space society on stations and on planet Mars."

"When we have accomplished some of these goals, Earth should be back to normal. We humans, in time, will have reeducated ourselves on how to live more compatibly with nature. When the time is right, some of you may return to Earth."

"Strict direction under the guidance of space science professionals is needed for our success and you must all learn to follow directions in masses. We are asking your support through protocard contract." Everyone has a card that vibrates an electro energy message of legal matters through the Ossoscan Recording Library (ORL). All votes, opinions and documentation is recorded through this library and is there for world viewing. This system can be transferred for use to space stations. "When the majority has registered their contracts with WRG," she says, "We will all begin to move. Any comments or opposition will be entered on the speed processors by the use of your ossoscan fibriolators. Adjust them accordingly."

Mr Muraste, Mr. Basade and Mr. Boschev are guiding a team of helpers to receive, process comments and opposition, then return them in condensed average form. This method is purely for the benefit of gathering ideas in a short period time.

Earth's surface substances are losing weight. The clatter and howling are reaching a state of nerve racking intensity. The ground and water is actually rumbling.

The team also has an instrument called the time estimating calculator which determines how much time is left before the weight of man lifts off the ground. They pro rate this information through to the people every hour. The last estimate was around forty five days. At that point in time, living beings will be able to leep into the air. That may seem like fun for awhile. The problem is this is getting worse and soon they will leep into the air and won't come back down without weights.

The people are now aware, because they trust the time estimating calculators, time is running out and they must have a better contract agreement. They don't want to be slaves.

The people have decided to let one of the Flintstock family be spokesperson on their behalf. They have chosen Luanne who has a broad perspective background and is dedicated to the cause.

Ms. Flintstock iterates a message to all the world on how the people must keep their autonomy:

"We've worked for centuries in bringing our state of compatibility together with trillions of people. We've learned trust has taken preference over suspicion and has kept us free of bondage. We will not give that up. It is up to us to take a stand. Our numbers, in masses of people, far surpasses that of the wealthy and elite. We have also learned using that power can move mountains. We will validate our protocard contracts for following the WRG's instructions to a tee in moving from Earth to the stations. We will further follow instructions in organizing our new colony in space. However, all this cooperation is subject to the WRG's agreement that allows our representatives to work on an equal basis with them toward our goals."

"We must remember these space stations belong to them on their property. Then we will initiate a transition from a passive society to a more affirmative society when the time is right for either returning to Earth or inhabiting Mars after we have learned new methods for survival."

"We will accept their promise to complete the details of our negotiations when we reach the stations. The impetus for this reasoning, based on trust, is the fact masses of people can be dangerous to a small amount of people who attempt to rule them. It is our intension for all of us to win together!"

The WRG has now received all the messages and is reluctant to agree and proceed with the mass transfer. If and when they all decide to move, the question arises how do they travel?

Interplanetary space travel now experiences smooth riding vessels made by WRG called whipstreakers. They exist in many sizes and are capable of approaching a clear target within one hundred percent accuracy. They are propelled by centrifugal force similar to that of a boomerang. The whipstreakers are motivated, on gravity based atmosphere, by nuclear reactors. When out of the atmospheric influence, they are motivated much easier by electrode positrating encomagnet inducer rays which extract energy from the sun and/or nearby planets. Once the vessel has gained momentum, from any beginning, inertia takes over for a smooth ride.

The ship's main body, exclusive of its power source, is a segmentational division joined by a large revolving bearing type connection controlled by one of the vessel's crew members.

The WRG wants more control over everything. They are very creative and helpful, but their thinking process is similar to that of being omnipotent. Their power status over others is in question.

This whole crisis episode seems to hindge upon scare tactics between those who think in terms of dominating and who think in terms of conforming.

Eleasa McKonkey has expressed a negative reaction to the people's representative. She states "absolute control will prevent arguing, fighting and errors. We cannot take the chance of chaos happening on the stations."

"We will all stay here until you have decided our way will suffice." Communication is closed.

A month and a half has passed and both sides are still deadlocked in their positions. Progress is still hammering away with energy influencing the atmospheric tendencies.

The ground is cracking which, in turn, is causing terrible destruction of infrastructure and general living conditions. The overall deterioration has been irreversibly eminent for several years.

More energy is used now in equipment for controlling the destruction.

While this is all happening, the rate of gravity degeneration is increasing and more people are beginning to panic; including the WRG.

Ironically, Mrs. McKonkey has reopened public communication just about the time Ms. Flintstock adjusted her frequency modulator on the ossoscan.

Mrs. McKonkey blasted Ms. Flintstock for contributing toward the destruction of mankind. "Who in the hell do you think you are leading all these people into chaos by resisting our plan to disembark from Earth?

"I'm no worse than you!" Ms. Flintstock returned. "Since we will all die at this rate, it seems kind of stupid and wasteful that we have come to the point of making strategic decisions all of which are based on emotional principles and fear."

"Yes—, it certainly does," Mrs. McKonkey says. "I mean yes, we certainly have."

"I'll tell you what," Ms. Flintstock states, "the reality is we will probably never come to perfect terms, so let us proceed to agree while we are in transition from traveling to and settling in the stations. We will put forth more effort in helping your cause to pilgrimize and settle our complex order of people. Whereas, you will maintain your "upper hand" while cooperating in our joint efforts to colonize a space society where we will all prosper socially from this endeavor."

Mrs. McKonkey peers out over her reading glasses, holds a straight face and says, "Terms accepted! Let's get going! The lift off of all these people will be accelerating the disembarking process. We must stay ahead of it all."

A broadcasted verbal agreement is considered a world wide socially accepted legal and vested contract and is honored by all.

Chapter 6

Some excape Earth's chaos and some don't

A great majority of the world's people are pleased in placing their confidence in Ms. Flintstock for helping to make final decisions. It appears most of the people have concurred with the agreement and have submitted that concurrence to the IWC and ORL whose facilities are barely holding together under the shaking circumstances.

Time is running very short and all the people are trembling along with the Earth itself.

The WRG has been slowly and meticulously arranging lift off vessels around the world for years with the expectation these or similar events of relocating masses of people would occur; all of which appears to be formulating in a similar manner they speculated.

Vessels are being filled with people, animals, food, water, money, credit, equipment and everything that can be loaded for promoting a society of living beings in outer space.

This is a similar repetition of the legendary Noah's arc only on a much larger scale both for reasons of survival and planning for the future. The big question is does it always work?

How do they handle trade with money? Precious metals are no longer used to back up currency. Currency is issued from good credit by the use of a credit card registering the degree of credit available at money machines situated in all public facilities. Spending, small or large, is accomplished by degree of credit qualification. That is, those who have the most credits gathered will qualify to spend or invest.

The rich really do not have to posses money in the amount of dollars as they did in previous centuries. They just have to build up or inherit credit which is considered a very high form of trust and the most powerful of dictates. This credit can be transferred anywhere.

Before the vessels are loaded, they are given instructions on where and how to board the ships.

Massive movements toward the vessels are occurring around the clock. Energy use is being overdrawn, the degeneration is increasing, the gravity is lessening and everyone is having to be especially careful in getting on board so they won't be injured or killed.

Ships are now leaving the ground. Ossoscan fibiolators function on low energy extracted from vessel static drag generated as they move through space. Everyone can communicate on them. The only thing needed now is to adjust their mean frequency modulators with minor calculations.

The formation of the ships are preplanned and guided by a system of flashing and fanning light displays. The lights are tracking modulators telling other ships (not their crews) which position to move into and/or stay. There is minimal verbal communication between the ships operators since most travel vehicles are engineered for program control. They also have manual override.

Massive groups of the space vessels are forming into position such that, in an encounter with asteroids, the chance of collision will be less than traveling in military formation.

Many days have passed for this total embarkation into space. The ships are hammering away through the debree which has ascended from Earth and occasionally one falls back to Earth with the loss of anywhere from fifteen hundred to three thousand passengers.

This sends fright and despair throughout the hearts and minds of others who witness it.

Chum Kong broadcasts a vote of confidence through all the ship's intercom. "Lift off is running within reasonable expectations. Casualties occur as in any mass traffic movement and should be considered normal under these life threatening circumstances."

The people of this era have experienced some deaths from accidents or hostility and it comes as a severe shock to them. It is right to save lives, but at the same time, is it right to allow expansion at the risk of losing lives?

Mr. Kong continues: "We will be transferring from Earth to the stations for several weeks and everyone must realize this lift off of so many people into cramped quarters of the space vessels is extremely difficult for all involved. We know this is the only way now and we must continue to concentrate on moving forward and not compromise." Debating the point slows progress and is avoided.

While travelers are still loading the vessels, the WRG spacecraft used are traveling from Earth to the stations at speeds of maximum capacities in transferring the majority of the population.

The WRG crews are becoming more proficient in their challenge to transfer many people in a short period of time and have about thirty five percent more to transfer.

Many people, in route to the stations and some who have reached them, have become ill from the changes and shocks they have been exposed to and are almost incapable of caring for the themselves. Insomnia, emotional phobia, cholera and other reactionary and self-induced diseases are a few. Thousands have submitted to helping each other in this critical transition from one lifestyle to another. Desperation and stench from illness overwhelms a new and determined society and many are dying.

There again though, in spite of the fact that progress in the movement is fairly good, the people are facing the dual reality of not only suffering pain from losing friends and loved ones, but of having to accept that death does reduce the population.

The waiting passengers on Earth have been applying weights to their bodies to prevent them from floating. They must stay inside buildings or next to heavy objects to prevent other objects and even humans and animals from hitting them while floating. Water and other liquids are heavier now and float through air in undetermined angles.

People opening their mouths can be slapped with a surprise that can choke them to death.

When a fire breaks out, the water may put it out and create a flood, but it also may trigger or increase other flammable materials to rage or even explode.

Any living being on Earth is extremely vulnerable and humans are still wasting time over possibilities of coping with the dilemma.

A few days of panic attempts to escape the chaos reveal many people are removing their weights and letting themselves ascend outward with a misconception they can float anywhere they want.

Big surprise! They are floating away from fire and liquids only to discover they are unable to float back down and are rising to their deaths when they are no longer breathing due to the lack of atmosphere and air.

Time has passed after much chaos on Earth and the last of the photocard passengers are on their way to the stations. What is left?

Half the population is determined, stubborn, greedy and die hard people who have chosen to take a beating and are "weathering the storm" by fastening weights to their bodies. They believe they will inherit the Earth for themselves after it has resumed to a less devastating state.

They have been told they won't survive. What they do not realized is they have placed themselves into an inextricable predicament of unsurpassable complications. They cannot excape Earth's reactions now even if they changed their minds. The WRG won't be back for a long time.

Floods are emanating from the ocean depths into the skies. Lighting bolts are striking everywhere. The Earth is shaking; adding to the heat energy influence on the atmosphere causing gravitational loss. The rising of water is heating up to a steam condition around the world killing marine life and many who are exposed to it.

Sure, this will all subside in time, but at the moment, there is a chain reaction occurring on almost all earthly functions and plains.

During time in space, this may be termed just another normal earthly reaction. After all, many unimaginable phenomenons have undoubtedly come to pass on this ancient planet over billions of years and who knows, maybe longer than that.

What seems important or even meaningful is the question of what is happening to those who chose to "weather the storm" or should we say "storm the weather" on planet Earth?

Their plan was to wait until the atmospheric and gravitational forces battle and cancel their own momentum; thereby shrinking all earthly functions to normal.

Several days have passed. People and other life are experiencing a real life threatening drama more frightening than they could have ever dreamed.

Degravitation is beginning to reach it's maximum stage with a constant howling of speeding debris along with the helpless and terrified screams of struggling humans and animals.

While the swirling hell of lightweight materials of dirt, rocks, water, oil, sewage, steam and fire are moving around and outward crashing into other debris, living beings are being battered and tossed around by the thousands. They are perishing from lighting, smashing injuries and ascension into space.

All the remainders can do now is wait their fate. Finally, after twenty more days and nights of hell on Earth, the peak of momentum has been reached. The world now has a ring of debris around it at a distance of about one hundred twenty miles out. Everything imaginable is there circulating planet Earth similar to that of Saturn except the moving pattern is unpredictable.

A good portion of the people left on Earth went underground. Some are in basements with supplies. Some had to dig caves underground and are surviving on deep rooted vegetation and small land and sea creatures.

Now the survivors of the world can take a breather. It is only a breather though, because with the degravitation coming to a peak, all the debris is beginning to return to Earth. It could be a smashing entrance!

The people who are aware of this inevitability are covering up and/or digging further under to prevent direct bombardment.

Just as the degravitation swings over the peak in momentum, the fall to Earth is hardly noticeable.

Very gradually, gravity increases in time and with it the speed of all the debris returning increases. The faster it all returns, which is time consuming, the harder the Earth and its inhabitants are hit. It's like one constant rain of debris until it all lands in places it wasn't particularly meant to be, at least from the human stand point.

Many moons will pass before Earth will be inhabitable again because of the unbalanced electro static atmospheric degeneration. It will take years to thoroughly equalize. The survivors are definitely not capitalizing on the real estate yet. They have all they can do to adapt to the adverse conditions their predecessors have left them with.

Weeks have passed again and the debris entering is somewhat less now. The survivors have been battered to the point of exhaustion. They have really been put to a test. They are weak now, but at the same time they have gained other strengths of how to survive and move ahead.

One of the not so greedy, but dedicated Earth survivors said staying on Earth may seem like a defeat, but to surrender it without a battle would be a worse defeat. So far, we have won."

If they had conformed to the WRG, obviously the ones who died may be alive now. That would appear lucky for them at the time, but would it help the population expansion?

Much can be said about the right, the wrong, the good, the bad, the just and the proper etc. concerning the control or preservation of life on Earth, but for now, dealing with what they have is the issue with the survivors.

Weeks have passed again with more gravitation returning. The people are aware they will become extinct if they don't use their bedraggled energies in a more than ever creative manner to colonize and rebuild a very tired and humble society.

There is still more than enough of everything needed to start a life again. It's just all rearranged in a completely unconventional and scattered array of junk over the earth. Most of the usable equipment left is nonoptional, at least for the present time. A lot of the debris and people ascended into an Earth's orbit and won't return.

The survivors have newly acquired courage to search and gather morsels of their fate to keep them functioning from day to day. They are able to get water from underground streams and pools. Unfortunately, sometimes they drown in them. They are discovering new sources of roots and herbs along with life under the surface of the Earth.

Many are still dying, injured, sick and unable to help themselves or others. Many are fortunate to be alive, but frustrated and angry because they have no one to blame for this state of chaos. Others weep with the thoughts of not returning to their previous lifestyle.

Many still cling to rebuilding their society. Some are accepting the status quo and others have given up.

Planet Earth has an innate and natural intelligence, in its aliveness and suffering of which mankind never really accepted. It either allows its surface to be disturbed or repels it. In repelling, this form of intelligence doesn't conform to reacting in such a way that may be understood by humans. It reacts in a way that can only be understood scientifically.

If that intelligence could translate that science into mankind's manner of understanding, mankind would know exactly what to do and what not to do concerning living in a state of equilibrium with that intelligence on a regular basis.

Mankind has probed and researched possible connections with that intelligence to resolve a compatible relationship between man and Earth.

Unfortunately and for the time being, man has been unable to resist his insatiable appetite to exploit the planet and tap it for all its energy.

This rerouted energy used, in the process of exploitation and in turning the wheels of progress, has adversely affected the atmosphere and has caused the gravitation chaos. Earth has become lighter weight from the ascending materials and veered away from its normal path around the sun to some degree for awhile.

The astrological effect of Earth's new traveling route around the sun is dangerously close to a dense asteroid belt between Mars and Jupiter. When they hit Earth, the survivors become subjects of extinction.

Presently, any life form entity interested in settling down on a serene and secure planet better think again about planet Earth. Viewing the present possibilities, this planet can be considered uninhabitable for now.

How do the survivors see it? It is about one and one half years after the gravitational ascending peak and normal gravitation has resumed. However, Earth is still somewhat off course. The orbit pull is in a drag state of momentum.

The remaining people have been through what could be considered the worst possible disaster they could ever experience and still survive. They are still whirling around the solar system in an unfamiliar state of space travel that is colder than normal due to Earth's present orbiting path that is further away from the sun.

Earth's survivors managed it and learned to dig into the ground for preventing exposure to the debris, asteroids and changing weather conditions etc.

While learning how to just survive, they come out occasionally to survey, scavenge for edibles, building materials and substances that can be used for fertilizer including cadavers.

They have learned life itself is just as precious to the individual as the materials of the Earth are in the makeup of the world and infringing upon that reservation has its heavy costs. They have not only learned the humility of losing loved ones and almost their own lives, but have also experienced exasperation from being greedy, stubborn and self-possessed.

Chapter 7

Station living and needs of Earth's survivors

During the same time Earth was passing through a critical period, the greater masses of people who have departed from the Earth and traveled to the space stations have been having their problems too. Many died in route similar to the people who were brought over the ocean to be used as slaves in the new world of the seventeenth and eighteenth centuries.

Moving such masses of people in space vessels was an extremely crowded ordeal. That condition taxed the vessel's energy sources for processing and transforming air, food, water and waste.

The stations are also massive. There are many of them which were built as a result of a thriving world society of people. They were built to be used anywhere in space. They are now positioned in an orbit between Mars and Earth, but closer to Mars.

They are arranged and planned so they can be repositioned in logical places for extracting energy from various scources in the solar system. Without that needed energy, they will fail to function.

The year is 2425. Time is a little different now on the space stations and all clocks are adjusted to a new orbit time around the sun. Days and nights are nonexistent; just small shadows from the stations. For the purpose of these writings, Earth time prevails.

The way of life is quite different on these space stations. Living quarters is closer than they have been used to and everyone has to cooperate and do their part to prevent panic and create reasons to live and maintain a new way until such a time they may move onto Mars or back to Earth.

The population on the stations is much less than original due to many deaths in transit, mishaps, miscarriages, panic and illness. The move hasn't been as horrendous as that on Earth, but has taken its toll on a weary and humble people including the WRG. In fact, the WRG understands they have to lessen their dominant stance on the people because they need their complete and voluntary support. They are discovering a people ruled are a people separated who may eventually run out of reason to excel. They are realizing they must all help each other with their pursuit of progress. They haven't changed in that.

Time has past and the station people have been able to pool their differences and form a fairly secure coalition for promoting the survival of living beings in space.

The people have the flexibility to move from one station to another for promoting the cause of surviving whether it be on the stations, Mars or back on Earth. They move from station to station in small capsules which are propelled by antiatmosphere vacuum through body sized space ducts. Space station living has its wonders, inconveniences and limitations.

The space stations are basically round like a fruit cake container with a lid on it, except on the station, the lid is part of the structure. There is no hole in the middle. They are made of a newly discovered material called trilythosparsoniam which can withstand reentry temperatures and inside pressure of up to five hundred PSI @ 14G.T. It is the lightest and strongest of all known substances. The station has various sized rooms throughout with shatterproof windows. Inner rooms are work stations without windows. There is a cylindrical shaped control headquarters extended through the structure from (in Earth's language) top to bottom with transparent bubbles on each end for viewing.

These stations are towed with shaft links which is a tube with connectors on both ends.

There are different size stations for different tasks. Their maximum capacity is ten thousand people and are self-contained with technicians and maintenance crews on each one.

They have all the necessities of home on board. The people are kept busy with, generally, planned activity of work, leisure or play.

Each station has a health and medical facility with two doctors and assistants. Whipstreakers depart and arrive through pressurized chambers on the two disc flat sides. The stations vary from two to four stories deep and are equipped with weightless offsetters (artificial gravity).

Living on these stations is similar to living on an ocean liner. Almost everything is available as long as they keep replenishing artificially and naturally.

Work on the Mars project has been almost nonstop since the evacuation of Earth and now the whipstreakers are speeding back and forth with more labor than ever.

Mars has been a store house for years of interspace equipment and space travel vessels. They are working on the planet for inhabitation in the near future.

The year is 2435. The majority of the people remain fairly optimistic about survival and developing their society where they will possibly inhabit Mars. However they also cling to the possibility of returning to their birthplace Earth.

Occasionally, they swarm together in small meeting places where the coalition airs out their anxieties and attempts to reveal everything known by the directors and observation groups.

"We have suffered and have lived in and on restricted areas for years now," says Barry Adler, one of the middle aged crusaders who worked with Luanne Flintstock on Earth. "We have adhered to rules because we know it's critical to do so. Now we need to hear a little more from you about where you believe we are going.

Questions are aired out what do the probes onto Earth reveal about the reversing process? Did anyone survive? When is it feasible to return to Earth?

A worker from the astro station answers: "All indications reveal you wouldn't want to visit or set up housekeeping there now. There are survivors, but the planet is being hit with asteroids from the direction it is moving around the sun and is experiencing extreme cold episodes."

"Your coalition is devising a plan to move a small station into orbit a safe distance from Earth for closer detection that will be capable of dodging asteroids. There are crews working on it steadily. It will be ready soon."

The crowd calms down a bit from their questioning, but now they are stirred up concerning one of their old habits; progress.

The air among these people is exciting and trying at the same time because no one really knows yet if they will recognize Earth after the disastrous effects.

They want less talk and more action. The more talk spreads of Earth probing, the more the people, without organized guidance meet to conjure up ideas of their own. Some of those ideas involve a coalition takeover which is mostly emotional blurting and not too reasonably creative.

Population reform has had priority on the station community planning agenda and has had majority compliance.

Even though the people do agree with rules and regulations concerning strict birth control and separating the population among the stations of Mars and Earth for a few years, they seem to have more of a passion that involves plans for returning to Earth.

Barry Adler had been arbitrarily chosen to accept responsibility in helping to guide a return trip to Earth. He now has to put the pressure on the WRG, IWC and people's coalition.

They have all formed more meetings exposing the pros and cons. The upper echelon advises waiting and becoming more educated before proceeding. In one of their primary meetings, their representative Mrs. McKonkey says, "It would be much wiser to think, prepare, look and wait before you leep!"

Mrs. McKonkey is verbally supported by astro station's Dr. Robbins who says, "Earth is not quite settled back to normal yet. Earth is resuming its original path slowly, but it is still vulnerable to asteroid attack. The atmospheric condition is still contaminated with Earth powders of radio active waste and other materials."

The people are not satisfied with that conservative and time consuming approach. "We've had enough stalling for promoting your space enterprises," says group spokesman Jaroldo Flores. "We don't want to work and rot here in this foreign place of space," he says, "We would rather take our chances on Earth. We have power in numbers. If this is what we want, let's use that power and present our vote to the WRG and IWC. It will take time to prepare and in that time, Earth will be closer to normal. If we wait and keep conforming with the Mars project, we may not have a chance to gain the initiative for returning to Earth. That's our planet. Let us not forget that!"

The meetings gather. The meetings break up. The people are using their power in numbers now and have submitted their votes to the echelon.

The votes are overwhelming for returning to Earth. The people know they are unable to harness a project of that nature without cooperation from the WRG and IWC unless they conduct a full fledged meeting and in this day of time, mass populations are not programmed to work against each other. The result is just as it was previously on Earth. Legislative procedure and final decision making is tossed back and forth similar to that of the so called peace talks of the Middle East back in the twentieth century. Sometimes they reach an agreement. Other times the status quo is stale and goes nowhere, but they don't quit.

The year is 2493. Earth has calmed down considerably with the remaining ring of debris back on the surface. Gravitation is fairly normal, but the original orbit path is taking longer to resume.

The people of Mars have been working, planning, arguing, crying and begging with each other to come to an agreement on Earth's reentry and finally have concurred harmoniously to leave half of the population on the stations and Mars project and return the other half to Earth. A preliminary fleet of ships will probe and test Earth before the masses return.

Hundreds of probing experts from all their prospective professions have gathered at the probe ships for departure to Earth. These people include technologists, scientists, geophysicists and medical experts. Scores of ships are being prepared.

The loading of equipment and supplies for this somewhat risky encounter has been unfolding like clockwork.

Everyone is exerting their natural and acquired skills to promote their cause of going back to Earth. In view of life style change, humans are becoming more obsessed and relentless in their efforts to gain what they thought they lost. Earth is their goal. Mars is second.

Chapter 8

Space travel to planet of enemies

The ships are lifting off the stations in single file formation through space which involves a planned route, eventually, around the Earth just out of the gravitational atmosphere. When arriving, they will begin the probe at Earth's doorway.

Speed doesn't seem critical now, so they "cruise" through the constant light of the sun.

They witness electrostatic discrepancy arrays about three quarters of the way to Earth on their space view screen. Magnifier focusing displays an array of scattered rock like appearances moving at an incredible speed.

The command ship's captain orders "All ships within .00820 range bank on seventy degree angle and face parallel direction with the foreign objects. Continue the direction until the objects have past. Use radmetic sensor buffers to maintain safe parallel distance from the objects."

The ships turn and glide alongside the objects. They can now more clearly be viewed as asteroids. Apparently Earth's atmosphere, having been thrown out of line created a rippling affect on the asteroid pathways and bounced the rocks in several directions.

Again, the captain orders, "All vessels upline of .00820 range begin a single SLT circle of 10-X coordinates and stand by for further instruction!"

Generally, spacecraft of this age in time are flown by private individuals. However, where strict discipline is necessary, as in massive flights, military guidance is used and strictly adhered to.

These asteroids are sporadic and difficult to detect until right on them and dangerous because of their speed. Size is no issue in view a small one can blow a ship apart as well as a larger one. Detected early enough, they can be somewhat avoided. However, there are thirty vessels riding alongside them. Four have exploded and six have been crippled and considered junk in space. The passengers on the disabled ships are injured and some are dying. As the coordinate circle is completed, the captain has not had directions from the WRG and IWC to return to the stations, so his commander on another craft sends the accident details to the medical station and they, in turn, lift off for rescue operations.

The asteroids have passed and the remainder ships have returned to formation which is a holding coordinate in the shape of a circle.

Military assistance has been trained for possible disasters and hold their disciplined focus, but the rest of the people are now shaken with fear.

When spacecraft or anything else collides while in orbit, it creates junk that tends to get pulled into the orbit or even outside of it and continues to move by virtue of inertia. This and even floating bodies can cause other collisions.

The rule has been established where the expedition return to stations will only occur if Earth is not fit to live on or if over half the vessels are disabled. The expedition moves on from the present circle coordinates.

A few days of moving through the monotonous, but beautiful heavens of space, have revealed floating Earth items escaping Earth's atmosphere and have mixed with the geocorona, a gaseous belt of ionized hydrogen at point of Earth's atmosphere. Passing through this friction of atom reactions has taken a toll of more ships resulting in more rescues and more cremations.

The remainder of the expedition trickles in on planet Earth's atmosphere. Readings and calculations from sensor instruments are recorded and analyzed. "Air contamination on Earth is still sixty five percent unhealthy" (one hundred percent is life threatening) said Dr. Sterns, an astro physicist on the intercom. "A spacesuit would have to be used to walk on Earth for safety," he added. "It also appears gravity is almost normal on Earth. It is still dangerous, though, without weights attached. I recommend waiting for awhile before descending.

All the acquired data is relayed directly to the station receiving by laser designator frequency. That frequency is "shot" in a direct on static line from the sending ship to its destination. That laser requires only one initial "shot" to propel it across space. Once it is received, the transmission ceases and any further communication must be "shot" again.

The vessels are circling the globe at about ninety miles out propelling on its own energy source with a humming sound in the familiar, but eerie skies of Earth. A dense, humid and dusty fog lingers propitiately around the globe as though it were purposely nurturing and protecting an injury.

Four primary objectives are sought after in this expedition. First, determine the state of safety to recolonize, second, determine if there are survivors, third, determine what condition they are in and fourth, determine what their responses and objectives are, especially in relationship to the incoming expedition.

Remember, when the people of Earth split up, the ones who decided to stay had a new attitude about the people who departed. They automatically assumed the Earth belonged to them and if there are survivors, they may not want to share their loot with those who ran away. There may be a distinct rivalry encounter that could lead to a geo/space conflict.

Some experts of this expedition are reserved about landing for awhile. The station people's coalition representatives aboard see it as unwillingness to take risks and face direct encounters.

Information for making decisions is sent by laser designator to headquarters.

The next few days are being filled with sleepless debate, arguments and constructive suggestions. Of course, everyone wants their own way.

Well, they are finally settling their ego driven differences by agreeing to pool all their suggestions with an analyzing machine which undergoes a complicated text of deductions, arrives at average answers and according to agreement, settles the debate.

The strategic decision making process on Earth would take months and maybe longer. Here on the space stations, though, at least at this time, all issues are moving along much faster.

The decisions are made. The director at WRG and IWC for landing on Earth is Chum Kong who sends the message to the fleet captain for landing procedure: "Earth and possible survivors will be examined, not exploited, first from a distance of one thousand feet. Remember, we may be considered enemies now. Send minimal crews in on capsulecars in equal positions of the world. Proceed nonaggressively and with grave caution."

Humans have done it again. They just won't leave the status quo as it is.

"Message received and understood," replies Captain Reynolds. "Lieutenant," the captain barks, "Arrange for fifteen capsulecars and reverse gravity equipment to descend." "Right away sir," he says.

Later, a crew of fifteen WRG experts are gathering to board capsulecars for passive scientific probe and human inspection.

The nonmilitary personnel are always a little slower in response, but they all tolerate each other with patience and cooperative attitudes. After all and generally speaking, mankind has always worked fairly well together in group activity.

The capsulecars descended to Earth in precise regimented form as far apart as they are. This way, the captain's instruments can record any discrepancy reactions while approaching Earth to determine if reversing is necessary.

Centuries ago, spacecraft landed horizontally. Now, almost all spacecraft descends directly onto the surface in a ninety degree angle to the surface.

The capsulecars land the same way. When they reach one hundred feet above the ground, they are allowed the flexibility of traveling in either direction.

All the cars have now touched down and the whipstreakers above are maintaining open frequencies for communicating with the cars.

The atmosphere and air is tested from inside the capsulecars. All cars are equipped with oxygen masks and weights for possible use on the surface of the planet.

Outside their capsulecars, which holds two people, they are astounded with their discoveries.

"I see no one around, reported one prober, just hills of regurgitated real estate, building fragments, industrial remains and shattered bones scattered all around as though they were run through a tsunami."

Giant holes in the Earth from asteroid attacks are seen from the ships above. Deserts and flatlands are still wet from oceans and lakes bathing them (remember, Earth is still somewhat off its orbital path and colder than normal which explains why the water hasn't dried up yet. Radio active dust and other contaminants are registering unsafe on the instruments and oxygen masks are fastened.

Conversation is kept to a minimum on the communicators. Everything observed is recorded on their transcorders which are automatically sent back to the ships above.

Others around the world are reporting similar aftereffects of devastation.

The probers who saw no one around are deciding to do some digging. They are more than just curious. They see what looks like footprints. "Daniel, check this out. The footprints stop abruptly," said the prober.

Suddenly, Daniel started to rise upward. "Oh my God! What's happening?"

A large cellar like door covered with dirt is raising up on one end. It moves higher and higher. Daniel jumps off and joins his friend to look inside.

"There's a flicker of light under the ground in the—." Before he could finish his sentence, they were both snatched into the ground almost as quick as they said oh! The door raised higher. In less than three minutes, the capsulecar vanished from sight. The door closed with a gush of dirt forming around the edges.

Captain Reynolds is notified one capsulecar has disappeared.

"Number four Daniel," his officer calls. "No response captain." Several requests to number four Daniel have had negative response. They were assumed to have been abducted.

Other incidences have occurred around the world on land where the people and the cars have disappeared completely.

Five hovering cars over the ocean have had virtually no activity other than wave fluctuation from Earth settling.

"Captain Reynolds to all vehicles. We are losing too many cars. All vehicles resume positions for immediate lift off." He no sooner completed his command than two more cars were plucked out of existence.

A few minutes reveals all the remaining cars around the world are off the ground and into higher formation.

"All cars reposition on a trajectory of forty five degrees at five hundred meters parallel," the captain ordered.

All cars verified their positions. The captain continues: "Rotate one quarter circum and propel for one thousand meters; then descend. This repositioning allows us inspection of completely different areas. Proceed with more caution." Again, human beings are obsessed with progress. They forge ahead with their determination and fears; good, bad or indifferent.

The cars complete their maneuver and once again descend to the surface. Cars over the ocean are now over land.

One car landed and immediately dropped through the roof of a covered underground passageway. Capsulecomm contact was lost and the two experts and car disappeared.

The other experts stayed in their cars and observed everything they could by day from their protected cars. At night, they returned to the whipstreakers and discussed their experiences.

From the whipstreakers, they can see occasional flashing lights on the Earth's surface. Remote photography shows the survivors have salvaged generators to manufacture light. That means they have the ability to manufacture other tools of progress.

Day break is here on half the world and formation begins again. This time orders are agreed upon to land in groups of three for possibly assisting each other.

There is much less coverage over the Earth's surface in blending with groups, but safety in numbers appear more important.

As previously planned, they all land at the same time and all appear to be safe. Those over the ocean continue covering wide areas and have seen endless floating debris.

One car observes no mounds of dirt, but another kind of disaster: "People couldn't be surviving here," said crewman Ivan. "The ground is muddy. Looks like a tidal wave hit and washed everything away. Looks pretty eerie."

"Yeah, like the lull after the storm," said his partner Anita as they stepped out of their capsulecar into the slippery and mucky ground to check out the area.

Suddenly, a roar of mud stomping people are rushing toward them. "Quick, back to the car," said Anita.

Just as they turn to run, Ivan's feet gets lodged in a mud hole. Anita is trying to help, but the muddy people are on them too quickly. They and the capsulecar are taken away.

The tracking crews above are aware the survivors are abducting the landing crews and their equipment. It is an obvious act of resistance or need. Maybe both. "All cars return immediately!" blurts the captain.

Now the expedition is clearly aware of what they were searching for and are almost in a panic to exit planet Earth having lost half of their landing resources.

All cars are now stored in the whipstreakers and the expedition is at an end. The main vessels will not be landing for now

Obviously, there is hostility lurking on Earth and the coalition is not prepared for war, so they turn in their direction and head back to the stations.

Chapter 9

Hazards of space and adapting to a new way

The stations are parked out of the gravitational pull near planet Mars. Mars is used as a guideline for general direction. The only problem is; moving in a straight line, like the crow flies, is generally a hazard with space fleets and they can be hit easily by asteroids in this area of the system. They can be hit even harder on their return to the stations because the asteroids are moving in the opposite direction.

The captain is a veteran of many exciting and hazardous episodes and a pro with celestial navigation. He, with his chain of command, holds the responsibility of jockeying through space toward their destination in such a way that prevents cataclysmic collisions.

So far, so good. The remaining vessels are heading off course twenty two degrees to avoid what looks like a gaseous trail from a small shooting star. Apparently this star was pulled into the solar system orbiting from an unprecedented arc in space continuum.

The gaseous trail blinds the visual controllers. The star is obviously moving ten times faster than the ship which fans a wider trail of gas as it moves.

Captain Reynolds consoles with his crew: "We can stay on a blinding route to avoid asteroids and maybe ride it out through the side of the trail as the star continues on its curve or resume our straight line route to the stations increasing the odds of hitting oncoming asteroids.

"Let's elevate on a forty five degree curve and go over it," states commander Orlaune. "Good idea," the captain says, "except we will then be in unacceptable parameters of our projected adjacent angle and to get back on our present speed might whip our vessels off course."

Two more officers say to slow down and drop off to the wayside and wait.

The captain explains, "We are on limited food supply already and need to get home. We could be conservatively cautious and starve to death in space."

"Okay, after all views are expressed, our goal is to return to the stations in a resourceful and reasonably rational manner which means we must perform a spiral trajectory maneuver. That requires a little more skill moving from a small funnel turn to a constantly larger funnel curve until we are clear of all hazards. This will take much less time and still keep us near our track."

"All settled? Let's do it," the captain commands. A series of numbers are exchanged, buttons are pushed and the show begins.

The ships turn over and around in a tight, twisting circle. The further they move into the trailing gas, the wider the circle becomes. The wider the circle, the clearer the view.

This maneuver reduces the odds of colliding with asteroids and allows them clearer vision while staying fairly close to the path home.

All the people on the vessels have been stressed to their limits, weary and famished. They have been so busy, they have ignored their well being. Almost everyone has stopped for a bite and have noticed the rations getting low.

While the vessels are escaping the asteroid threat, they have time to ride the long straight line to the stations and do some ship integrity analyzing.

Vessel one reports "encomagnetic inducers have burned excessively over accepted capacities. Further use may result in breech to burnout."

"Vessel eight reporting structural surface weakening from unknown scource at present. Bulkheads flapping against stiffeners. Pressure is decreasing slowly.

"Three other vessels have reported similar incidences," says Captain Reynolds, indicating all the space travelling has pushed their ships' resources to their maximum especially after all the activity they have been put through since originally departing from Earth years ago."

"Absolutely. They need renovating captain," says the chief in charge of mechanical functions.

People are transferred, in case of moving vessel deterioration, personal and visitor meetings, into body sized capsules from one ship to another through connecting vacuum tubes. Remote control turns off all evacuated ships and releases the tubes into the stable ships.

"Well," the captain remarks to an officer on the comm, "We've lost some more ships! What next, pirates from outer space?" The captain is joking in his frustration because he knows there have been no incidents of living celestrial beings in his career or before, at least not in this solar system. He believes, so far, human beings are the only living madness who have sailed this system with grandeur mentality to conquer.

Is mankind really ready to attempt conquering and inhabiting another planet?

So far, mankind has stretched their pretentious, determined and gullible minds as far as to think they could conquer planet Earth and made a mess out of that. How could they conquer any more? Apparently they think they can.

After a venture of unforeseen hazards, the team arrives at the stations weary and a little less enthused about reuniting on planet Earth, at least for now. All they want to do now is rest, eat and thank their "lucky stars" they are alive.

Many months pass and are turning into years with project Mars slowing down to an unproductive pace. The people are worn out from working hard, living on artificially induced food and suffering anxiety of believing they may not live long enough to resume a life on Earth.

The population problem is reducing, but it is more of a result of space venture fatalities and illnesses than it is from birth control. The lifespan is much less now resulting from these problems. The old adage "things have a way of working their way out" may apply here.

There was a time, in past decades, when the people actually tinkered with the idea of letting elderly people expire in a natural manner as compared to extending their lives artificially or even in a natural manner.

Now, they are beginning to realize life and progress is precious and needed, but reality of destiny is facing these people more than it ever has. The very thing they seem to need is the thing that is defeating them. They are beginning to perceive life as a concept of appreciating what they have and living in harmony with nature. Since they are out of touch with the nature they were exposed to at one time, they are changing their views. This is not just the people, but the leadership too.

If they survive by accepting and adapting to a different and foreign way of life and if they consolidate their beliefs by their realizations and if they are successful in maintaining a state of harmony with nature on Mars, a fair percentage of them may extend into future generations.

The question is not how much progress mankind will promote and/or acquire, but whether this ambitious and desire oriented flock of people will survive at all!

The Mars project continues, but is taking its toll in lives and other resources of which came from Earth.

A list of questions concerning mankind's destiny or doom could span around the planet of Mars and all be valid at this time.

The year is 2498. The people are tending to run out of steam and by virtue of their programmed heritage, they are just not willing to let it happen. Their beliefs have been so instilled in them where they possess an almost uncontrollable and instinctive urge to promote their cause regardless of the odds. Its almost like they can't die until it's done.

When planet Earth was overpopulated, they had everything they wanted except room and the satisfaction or fantasy of it continuing forever.

Now, they suffer the anguish and pain of breakdown in massive numbers. The space society is deterioration, but determined in a die hard sort of manner to fulfill a man-made destiny; a progressive society of space beings. That desire is like a pounding heart throb of euphoric desire staying alive with the insecurity life has to offer along with any or all the amenities.

The year is 2514. The people are still struggling, intermittently, in accepting their environment "as is" while also learning how to deal with and tolerate increased death incidences due to lack of future incite required in preventing them.

These deaths appear to be somewhat of a normal phenomenon now and the people are becoming emotionally tough in accepting this inevitable reality while also expressing the humility of loss.

All is not complete gloom and doom though. Human beings always look forward to something new.

A general meeting of the people and the echelon is revealing what progress means to them now.

"We were fools on Earth," says Barry Adler, Luanne Flintstock's friend. "We were fools to think we could promote successful progress by running away and we were fools to attempt a return as we did. Why has it taken us so long to see and understand why our system of progress was about to break down when we could have fixed it before it happened?"

"Our state of viewing reality needed therapy many many years ago. Let's do it now, before we wither away and become junk in space!"

"If we want to spend time promoting, promoting, promoting, why not use those energies in promoting the bottom line priority for the human race, which is to form a strict and stable governmental society compatible with nature's environment.

That means, rearrange the use of our energies available, pass legislation that helps, if not conquers desire, pass legislation we can agree will force us, if necessary, use the discipline needed to promote these new goals, pass legislation on what is preventive, not desirous, pass legislation that overrides and corrects flaws and mistakes of legislation and do it all before it gets out of control!"

The people listening on all the stations and Mars responded with an extremely noisy ovation of approval. It registered high on the decibal instruments. If they support this inspiring display of reasoning and if the people engage and marry this philosophy, they have a good chance of surviving and participating in the destiny of, at least, "our" solar system.

Whether it is the runaways in space or the leeches on Earth, humans always seem to want more at almost any cost and where has it gotten them?

Those in space were a mix of ambitious, greedy and scared people. A harsh lesson has rendered them humble, weak and definitely more perspective. Nevertheless, they still have a chance to keep the species alive and possibly improve their relationships with influences and forces of nature in our solar system.

Planet Earth is fairly quite now. The waters of the world have settled in their natural paths of resistance. On the surface, there is more salt in lakes and rivers from the oceans. The very few animals and insects surviving, which were very few, have adapted to the changes as they have for billions of years.

Mankind, being an intellectual species of beings, is surviving, but has had to become accustomed to living the adverse life of a mole. Moles prefer that life. Man doesn't, but they did it to survive the ultimate chaos. Mankind had no choice but to adapt to this way of life for the present time.

So far, most of the people of the world appear to agree, in salvaging some of their communications equipment, their primary objectives are to maintain good health by staying away from outside contamination and learning how to consume underground edibles and water while slowly adapting to the outside and accepting an extremely different way of life from their past.

They also appear to agree preventing or rearranging natural functions such as earthquakes, tornadoes, floods, asteroids and even comets are more of a long term nuisance than any geophysical benefit and to let them be as they are.

Their ongoing plan is to remain a family of people who will work together in all ways to prevent a repeat of recent history.

One broadcast in another part of the world, after time consuming and very creative communication equipment repairs, reveals "Our survival as human species is dependent upon preventing a repeat performance," says Charles Norton, a business executive. "We could have achieved this before the chaos if the majority hadn't gone into panic leaving Earth. From this time forward, we must vow to make workable rules and stick with them."

"If the station people return," he continues with anger, "We must let them know we did "weather the storm" and inherited the Earth by doing so. If they want a piece of it again, they cannot just come back thinking everything is the same. We must commit to being firm with them. None of us have negotiated their return to Earth. They all agreed to be space people and settle Mars. They abandoned us. This is no longer their home," he added. "If they return, vengeance is ours in any form needed at the time!"

People disagreed thinking the station people probably made mistakes, were sorry for them and they should be allowed another chance to reconcile. However, the majority who "did" communicate seem to stand fairly firm in their displayed convictions.

Their analysis and instinct to survive, at this point in time, has reminded them of their problem with acquiring food and may continue for some time until the people have evolved through the necessary stages of surviving a world disaster and sharing with the diserters is not in the interest of Earth people. They are living in a somewhat primitive manner at present, give or take a few acquired assets, from the time of their progress and are primarily concerned about the people on Earth, not the people on the stations.

Remember again, humans are humans. They always have been and just may always be ego driven, self-obsessed while community minded, possessive and incessantly hungry for security and power in any form they can acquire it. According to them, they will support their firm convictions until such a time it becomes more rewarding to change.

Chapter 10

Exploiting Mars and creating friction on Earth

The year is 2528. Change is slow, which is unusual for humans. Little by little, Earth's people are coming out of their man-made caves and learning to live on the settled down surface. They have graduated from consuming roots and underground water to surface grown vegetation.

Their adaptation to their changing world is a typical example of starting all over again. They are humble and pure in their efforts to allow nature to help them. They are learning to conquer procreation through practicing abstinence. They tend to the gardens which grow naturally and add to them. They let the land thrive as it was meant to and they are also cleaning up the mess of chaos and building up again.

Everybody works and finally some are expressing their inherent tendencies to play and express humor.

The kids are showing signs of normality by getting into little spats of trouble like they used to and they are searching for new kinds of pets they weren't accustomed to.

The adults are telling jokes again and putting on small stage plays from building wreckage.

Morale is picking up and the human spirit is coming back. That human spirit can be knocked down, but not really knocked out.

Back on the stations, physical activity here and on Mars has reduced considerably because of weakened human strengths and dragging motivation. The population has diminished close to thirty five percent through lack of life sustaining means of which could have been acquired from Earth such as real food, medicine, herbs etc.

The original people of the WRG and IWC have been long gone and have been replaced with their descendents and other ambitious folks. With new blood, there is determination to promote the cause of which humans are so good at.

The WRG and IWC coalition has a new title. It is called Tricoal. It exercises parliamentary procedure and has goals to colonize Mars and promote space activity.

They are very ambitious in spite of their problems almost like their parents were on Earth, except they do have the population problem in check and they know they must keep it in check especially for space minded people who are still in the pioneering stages.

Their immediate goal is to build stamina back into their people. Without it, they may perish from mal nutrition with all their aspirations incompleted.

Committee meetings and mass communication is a way of life on the stations and here is one of them:

"The time has come again," says professor Paul Kalenski who has recently been elected to lead the committee on surviving for future projects, "When we are faced with a serious problem, only going to Earth will solve it. If we don't get real food that comes from the ground, we will be in grave danger of extinction. True, we are in the process of directing Mars into and orbit that will allow the planet to function as Earth does, but we are not there yet."

This committee leads, temporarily, all activity on the stations and Mars and has been given authority by the people to guide their destiny in such a manner that will bring the strengths needed to promote their goals.

The work on Mars is not preparation primarily for the purpose of setting up immediate housekeeping. It's far from that.

The people work in special built in atmosphere suits and live very artificially while on Mars. The atmosphere is not supportive for humans and there is no food like humans are accustomed to. Moisture is extracted and manufactured from deep inside the surface of the planet.

What they are doing is digging giant holes for nuclear explosions on different angles to that of the surface to be used as propulsion caves when they are ready to propel Mars into an orbit around the sun equal to that of Earth.

Each hole will house a nuclear explosive. When it is detonated, it will spin the planet toward the direction of its targeted orbit. When it reaches its target, a series of complicated controls will keep the planet constantly reversing back and forth until it settles down similar, in results, to that of breaking in a young horse.

The theory is when the planet adapts to its new orbit, the atmospheric conditions will be equal to that of planet Earth and Tricoal will exploit it for colonizing.

Professor Kalenski continues: "I have chosen a team, including necessary military personnel, technicians, medics and workers, to fly to Earth and get food and supplies we need."

"The question has lingered for some time, whether this is the right thing to do or not. We have come to the conclusion it is! We are earthlings and that planet is ours too. The people there may not agree to that now, but over a longer period of time, they will. They will realize circumstances which were beyond our control at the time split us up, but we are all the same people in this space and time. After all, we may need each other even more at a later time than we do now."

"Presently, we are preparing a more strategy oriented move onto Earth. We will spend some time cultivating and growing crops and raising small animals. We will make it clear to the existing people this is only temporary and we will be gone in a couple of years or so. We will be going there in peace and hope they will realize we deserve, at least, a temporary portion of the planet."

"If they resist, we are prepared to demonstrate the power of our nuclear explosions we have been working with on Mars for digging holes."

"Our intentions are not to hurt anyone; only to display we are desperate. We believe we have rights and we mean business."

The year is 2531. The old whipstreakers are rejuvenated and have started to leave the stations in the same asteroid proof formation.

A new captain is now in charge by the name of Martin Hastings. One hundred and forty vessels are on the move this time and are equipped with more military and plenty of explosive materials for aggressive action or self-defense.

Since wars have been obsolete for centuries, war equipment has not been available to either side. Hand guns are only used by military and police officers.

The officers of the stations are well organized as compared to the people on Earth, but Earth's people have the advantage of more people for use in their defense against the travelers. Massive station people are not traveling to Earth this time; just a few hundred farm workers and technicians.

The vessels cruise and whip around obstacles through space in preparation for landing on a hostile planet and are practicing repeatedly as they maneuver around a stream of Earth's loses in space. This time their skills are more polished and they finally enter the long and somewhat intense path to Earth's outer stratosphere.

Moving into Earth's atmosphere happens fairly quick moving at forty thousand miles per hour.

The time is approaching for set down. This time, the crews are alerted, as planned, to form large circles of twenty ships in each to the best designated areas of the planet for agriculture.

Before setting down, printed fliers of intentions are dropped in a very wide area around the landing sights, hopefully, to prevent hostile encounter. The fliers mentioned explosive retaliation upon resistance. If such acts occur, other groups may assist.

Groups are setting down at intervals. There are a few scattered people noticed on the ground.

"Packages released," said Commander Conners, "Descend to ground and let propulsion idle until notified."

The landing is complete and half the ship's crews step out and cover the grounds to check for opposition.

An hour has passed with no resistance. Two hours. Three hours.

"This is too easy," the commander commented. "Be ready for anything."

The terrain is somewhat hilly and brushy in this area and difficult to see everything or anybody.

"Well, it appears the people are keeping their distance," the commander said. "Begin unloading."

While they started unloading the ships, they noticed what looked like clouds of dust swirling close to the ground. They could hear shuffling and hitting sounds.

Around the bend and through the trees, a herd of people appearing like thousands are running with sticks, pans, guns and clubs of different types toward the group.

"Stay in the center of the circle close together," announced the commander. "All ships elevate. Number two and four proceed to move toward the crowd."

Loud speakers trained on them said, "Our intentions are peaceful. Read the fliers. If you approach at your present speed, you will be considered hostile and we will drop explosives on you."

"We plead with you, Stop! Stop! Stop!" They continue thrusting forward with their almost out of control momentum and suddenly slowed down, stopped and scattered like ants to the explosives dropped near their threashold.

Some of them continue forward yelling, "Let's take them."

Most of them, being survivor oriented weren't ready for mass slaughter and came to a stop. The more aggressive ones were reminded by more explosives; they too must stop.

"The fliers tell you to stay away and do not interfere with our efforts," broadcasts the commander. They linger back slowly.

Two groups on the other side of the world have encountered no resistance from the people after they read the fliers with knowledge they didn't have offensive weapons sufficient to resist explosives.

Two groups in an Asian area of Earth are overwhelmed with increasing humidity which has lasted from Earth's calamity a couple of centuries ago and the land is rich for planting, but they need a plan to survive the wet air.

Another group landed a few miles from a well known city in North America. A large segment of survivors live there and battle the groups in numbers in spite of the explosives. There are more guns in this area which is raising havoc on the group. A battle, characteristic of desperate rivals, infringed on the peace that could have prevailed over the thousands of people killed on both sides including the loss of ships.

The last group landed in Europrussia, which is a nation centuries ago comprised of Europe, Russia and their neighbors. The group not only found a good reception, but made a deal to be share croppers working together. Both sides were scavenging to survive and agreed they needed each other to accomplish goals.

The people of Tricoal were aware their communicators may not function completely around the world and to land all in the same place, if defeated, would end their chances of completing their goals and might possibly mean the end of Tricoal and its people. Separately, they may have chances of establishing bases for farming. Eventually, they would fly from one base to another assisting where needed. Sometimes, this assistance arrives too late.

Tricoal may accomplish their mission with determination, skill, patience and luck. Alternatives are open at this time.

Chapter 11

Aggressive rivals and their differences

Year 2533. The earthly evolution of man has perceptibly reached an end only to begin again. Mankind will never again settle for being just "earthly." Man's space evolution has begun and although there will be many "astronomical" risks involved, their appetite to expand cannot be limited to one place. It is obvious now; Earth is just not enough.

So, there is a human destiny in space and mankind is an integral part of it. They are now projecting to prove it.

Man has learned how to learn on Earth. Now, they are learning why he is learning. He is forging ahead and stumbling through his new evolutionary education of his expansion in space because that's what the universe is all about; expansion. Earth was just too inhibiting. The question keeps popping up; are they ready for that expansion?

Mankind still does have a choice of limitations. They can stay a mole in a hole or an object in the shadow. They can stay at home and be satisfied. They can settle for working the land and living in harmony with nature. That existence with nature can be the paradox of human progress that raises the question where do I "want" to go from here? Better still, where "must" I go from here? How about where "can" I go from here?

What is happening with the farms? The world is a big place without an over burdening population and because of the size, there is plenty of room for everyone now.

The survivors and Tricoal are compatible in some areas and clash in others. The nature of the beast?

The Earth's survivors haven't been as well organized as Tricoal and now, since Tricoal has reached some of their goals of gathering food and supplies, the earthlings feel raged where the station people will be taking something away from Earth. They are gathering in groups and talking in terms of keeping what they believe is theirs.

"They came here with ideas of deception. They said they would only be here temporarily," states a large city mayor. They have exploited us and our land. They are taking food, grain, seed, fertilizer and even dirt. You know they can't move all that at one time."

"They will be whipstreaking back and forth at their leisure for years," he says.

"They either will control us or we will control them. Which will it be? If we want to gain strength and organize for controlling our Earth, now is the time to do it!"

The crowd, at this particular city, stomps up and down with rages of approval.

"Let's combine what little technology we have, conquer theirs and move ahead to create a better Earth for those who love it! We have the numbers. Let's use them now!"

The survivors have decided to wage war on Tricoal. Tricoal has been storing supplies for lift off for months and have felt tension growing between them and the survivors.

The word among the survivors is spreading around the world to organize for take over. The word also gets through to Tricoal.

"We have to leave now." One group security officer tells the commander. "It's better to leave with some than to not be able to leave." Everyone agrees and rapidly prepares for departure. "We must pretend everything is normal or they might rush us," the commander relayed to his group. "While doing so, everyone prepares to depart!"

Similar incidences are occurring around the world and lift off is imminent.

The original plan was, in the event of an emergency lift off, the craft would propel eastward to the next group and alert them, on the ship's communicators, to depart if they hadn't already began. They wouldn't land. They would just pass by and proceed to the next one etc.

Then all crafts would meet in atmosphere coordinates for the trip back to the stations.

This time, Tricoal is prepared to move quicker to prevent a repeat performance. "We can always come back and get the rest of it," comments a Tricoal member.

All the vessels are packed and uniting, without much incidence, to the coordinates and falling into their directed formation.

"I'm only sorry," says Captain Hastings, "All the ships and crews aren't returning to the stations. We are returning with one hundred twenty fully loaded vessels. Good luck to all of us." Earth's atmosphere dust has subsided greatly, thereby allowing a gorgeous three hundred sixty degree celestial viewing.

Weeks of normal boredom allows these space venturers a chance to rest and gather their wits.

Based on the previous trip to the stations, preventive measures have been undertaken where they have at least alerted the travelers for surprises which have been few this time. All captives have become Earth's subjects.

The ships are again approaching the stations. The shape of the formation changes, this time, from offset staggering to straight line up for smoother branching into their perspective stations. All vessels connect on their gusset perches and are pulled into small housing tubes which are then pressurized.

The ships are unloaded and the loads are placed for immediate use and storage. Most of the travelers are taking a brief time for reorientation and lunch. Afterward, the planning begins again.

Tricoal officials have also gathered for a real food feast and discussion on procedure to retrieve the balance of their goods from Earth. Food is served.

"Oh, is that ever good," remarked one official, "corn muffen dumplings and succotash."

The main speaker of Tricoal at this meeting is Professor Kalenski, who is relating on surviving for future projects. "We all deserve this feast," he says, but we must also pull our resources together for retrieving what is ours on Earth."

"Until such a time, after rerouting Mars and we are able to grow our own crops on real land, we are dependent on these sources from Earth."

"Guided by our military, we may be required to annihilate large segments of people on Earth if we believe we will be attacked.

"Let's face it, if both sides have reached a point of no return, it is either them or us. Which side are we most concerned with?"

A vote is taken, after much debate, on using aggression if necessary without intent of take over. The vote will be approved or disapproved by the people of Tricoal.

The equivalent of three weeks have passed and a very speedy voting has been completed. The people have concurred to use excessive methods if necessary.

Fliers are being printed stating: "We are returning shortly to pick up our food and materials we worked for. Please make it your business to secure its existence where we left it. Since you have been hostile with us, it becomes necessary to warn you if you deprive us of the food and materials we need to stay alive until Mars is inhabited, masses of your people will be extinguished by larger nuclear explosions. No further notice will be displayed."

Tricoal's plan is to send two ships to Earth prior to the main fleet, drop the fliers, return to space close to Earth and wait until the fleet arrives and observe the ground activity. Then all will proceed for the pickup or aggressive action.

The people of the stations are aware they must hurry and pick up the food and materials. If they don't get there in time before the Earth people snatch their goods, all hell will occur.

The flier ships are now preparing for the new flight. One week later: "Proceed to eject all vessels," said the captain on all stations com. "Check your sequence variables."

One hundred sixty vessels are moving out toward Earth this time with enough explosives to stop the resistance of Earth's people. That's one thing Tricoal has plenty of; kick and push!

The flier ships have delivered their flier loads and are back on coordinates waiting for the massive flights to arrive.

Time again has passed and the first and secondary vessels are uniting over Earth.

"You all know your destinations. Break formation and good luck," says the captain.

Twenty explosive vessels are circulating Earth with open communicators and ready to strike on minutes notice.

Many of the survivors around Earth have decided to pool their arsenal of guns and use them against the station people. They are capable of making cartridges and have been stock piling them.

Their thinking is if they can concentrate enough shots on one vessel, they will destroy it especially if it contains explosives.

What they don't know is the flying height is well over a mile and their bullets are not real effective at that distance.

Well, some one has to attempt a landing first, so two unmanned and unarmed capsulecars are being sent down on remote control over the area near a well known city in America. The cars are reaching an elevation of five hundred feet and are being riddled so full of bullets; the cars are falling to the ground in pieces.

"Prepare explosive detonators on target number one, two and three," directs commander Collins. "Release number one." This one was dropped over the crowd who shot down the capsulecars. They annihilated them instantly.

A back up group witnessed the incident and retreated to the city swiftly.

Industrial nuclear explosives are the only type available in this time of space and have been designed to where there is no fallout contamination. "Descend to objective sight for pickup," said the commander.

A few thousand miles to the east in the Europrussia area of the globe, people aren't nearly as unfriendly and no explosives seem necessary to use. However, most of the food and supplies have been moved to other unknown places.

Now, it is the decision of the professor and the captain to proceed aggressively, objectively or abandon the mission.

A ship's conference reveals possibilities: Landing without knowledge is too risky. Flying low is also too risky. Not landing will mean no food. Lower capsulecars are in different spots with the question written on them "what will it be, peace or war?"

Without delay, the decision is made. "Attach the signs and begin to lower unmanned cars," affirms the commander to the crew. "First, number five to the midst of the crowd at my command," he states.

After the surveying and calculation strategy, the word is given "descend to objective slowly." The car sets down on, what looks like, an organized mob just above the ground enough for them to see the note. The people are running around again like scattering ants yelling and raising their arms with hand gestures. Several people are running off into the distance like they have a definite objective. In a few minutes, they return with a large note waving it in the air to the vessel above.

"It appears they are sending us a message," says the ensign. "Lower the car," says the commander.

A man on the ground fastens the note to the car and it is pulled to the vessel.

It says, "We worked with you before. We will try again. Land your craft and leave us explosives in exchange for your supplies."

Before the chaos, the original WRG bought explosives from the manufactures who were in this area and sent them to the stations.

Talks above are underway and pointing to a possible agreement between the two potential business associates.

"What happens at this spot on Earth may determine future relationships between us," says Professor Kalenski to commander Collins. "Agreed," said the commander, "It looks like we have to take a chance. Send one ship down."

All those listening agreed. One ship only is descending to land. Everyone is tense on both sides. Can they trust each other? Suspicion and optimism is running high.

When Tricoal steps out of the ship, thousands of people gather around. A representative from both sides meet with no handshakes or hugs. This can be vicious business.

"We will give you a one thousand CM preparation for each shipload of food and supplies which will be lowered from ships above when ships below are loaded," yells the representative from Tricoal.

"We want two thousand CM," cracks back the ground representative. Tricoal tells them: "Accept the offer or we will both lose more than we want to lose."

They split the difference with a verbal agreement of wanting to do business together in the future. The loading begins with one ship at a time.

Each twenty ship encounters for food and materials are confronted a little differently. Three are easily accomplished. Three are devastatingly difficult with debates and arguments over who gets what.

"What you're giving us," said a Tricoal forman, "is a shipload of inferior quality. Take it back and replace it with the best."

"It's all the same," replied the supplier.

Both sides are overwhelmed with emotion and begin fist fighting.

There were many injuries and Tricoal realized the food was old, but they had to accept it.

Still, in another area, it's slow and nerve racking due to underground defiance. That is, some people have chosen to live their lives more underground than above and Tricoal finds it difficult to locate the supplies. Persistance, along with the threat of explosives, allows diminishing resistance and finally access to the goods.

Weeks have passed and the ships are now flying in the agreed direction whereby they will all eventually come into formation for Earth's departure.

The empty and unconquering ships are doing follow-up loading, then ascending to join the fleet. Most of the ships returning to the stations have a plentiful sized load. The mission did cost several thousand lives on both sides and two unloaded ships which were ambushed with gunfire causing chaos and creating more enemies.

The fruit of their endeavors on both sides was costly. Both sides profited, within their own contentions and both sides endured the hardship of losses. Around the world, both sides made friends and both sides made enemies.

Where will all of this confusion go in the future? The future is a representative of past preparation. Where has that gone?

There is an action as always; then a reaction. That, of course, is one of the basics of physics in the universe. When all mankind is constantly aware of this psychological phenomenon, reactions will still occur, but they will favor resolution over continuity similar to that of twenty third century legislation.

While the morale and fortitude of the Tricoal crews is teetering somewhat, this whole encounter between all of the peace loving people of planet Earth has left all of them dismayed in their accomplishments.

They realize there are wide sociological and now geographical gaps between the survivors of Earth and the station people.

The wide gaps are;

1. Earth's survivors still feel like Earth belongs to them. The station people feel like they can return any time they choose.
    Earth's survivors will fight them if they do.
    The station people will construe that as aggression.

2. Earth's survivors have been beat down to where they can accept more of a rudimentary lifestyle. The station people are still more scientific and progressive in their ways.

   The survivors are only interested in surviving. The station people want to develop and move ahead.

3. The survivors are somewhat conscious of preventing procreation, but overpopulation is not an issue now.

   The station people have developed a strong and controlled stance on prevention.

   The survivors don't want to be concerned about preventive methods.

   The station people are constantly aware of abstaining.

4. The survivors don't want to share with overpowering people.

   The station people's demands are justified by contentions of surviving.

The survivors feel like they have been invaded.

The station people feel like Earth is theirs too.

5. The survivors could care less about living elsewhere in space.

   The station people believe in expanding throughout the solar system.

   The survivors wouldn't know how.

   The station people wouldn't tell them.

   The only thing they both agree on is:

   The survivors hate the station people and the station people hate the survivors; at least for now.

Year 2538 the weeks have passed again and the Tricoal people are approaching the space coordinates of the stations.

"Captain Hastings," called Commander Collins, "We are approaching the three coordinates, but the stations just aren't there!"

"What on Earth is going on," questions the captain. "Rotate the comviewer and send a message requesting position," he commands. The comviewer is a high frequency, variable adjusting radar communications detector capable of audio video reception up to approximately fifty thousand miles through and/or around material substance.

"Captain, I have them," the technician says. "Station number twelve here," says the lieutenant on the comviewer. "Incoming ships request your position," states the technician. "The stations have repositioned on the opposite side of Mars sir, at CO 76876.02 by 9.5.

The ships must now follow an engineered and prescribed path so as to arrive at precise coordinants which allows safer station connections on the night side of the planet.

Tricoal has always parked near the planet on the sun side in a semistationary position for easier access to all areas of Mars as it turns. Now they are on the dark side.

Stations are approached and connections commence with all lights on. All connections are safely secured.

From this point on, everyone breaths a sigh of relief again, rests for awhile and begins unloading while officials proceed with their usual progress updating meetings.

The first meeting is to clarify and discuss reasons for the station moving. After the usual red tape procedure, the speaker of committee on moving Ben Muraste, son of Anastas Muraste, says, "We found we were having the same problem Earth has in a heat spell, only much worse. After Earth moved temporarily off its normal orbit, there was a delayed energy action whip wave that rolled over Mars creating the planet to move slightly toward the sun. This also meant the stations had to move over and in turn create a detrimental heat ambience on the stations which required moving around the back and trailing side of the planet. This may be permanent. We don't know yet.

Mr. Muraste finishes up with "the reason for originally locating on the sun side was, obviously, for the benefit of constant working light and a closer orbit to that of Earth."

"Now the problem is," says Professor Kalenski, "it will be twice as difficult to get Mars ready for reorbit. It means more delays and sacrifices. It means possible mistakes and casualties while working in the dark. It may mean possible defeat in our objective to reorbit Mars and that would mean we would all have to return to Earth."

Tricoal's echelon meetings usually have last choice in making decisions. However, this decision will affect every single person on the stations, so the people have the right to decide what they want to do.

The system of voting is almost the same as that on Earth. The crusading procedure begins.

"We have worked, fought and suffered too hard just to give it all up. Let us decide to pool even more of our resources and efforts and work harder to accomplish the risky, but potentially very rewarding plan of re-orbiting Mars." Several speakers voiced their opinions.

Chapter 12

Conflict over movement of planets

After a series of computations and calls are completed, the final tabulations have resulted in concurring to go ahead with reorbit.

Such is the human grandeur of Earth's most determined and intellectual creatures. They forge ahead relentlessly, promoting their most prized possession; progress.

They do that, of course, thinking it's for the survival and betterment of mankind. It is unheard of them to just settle for being, especially since they have acquired such an advanced breed of promoters capable of splitting the atom, splitting the household, splitting the earth and maybe even splitting the solar system.

Oh, they are great! Give them enough time and they might even expand the universe to a crummy pile of waste that won't even explode any more. How rewarding. Guess what.

Mars has been realigning to its original path, Tricoal has returned to its original coordinates on the sun side due to Mars resuming its original path and they are dramatically preparing to trigger a movement of this slaved over and exploited heavenly body to move it over even more.

The people have distributed their food and supplies and are back working on Mars diligently. Months are turning into years again and they have made trips back to Earth with similar clashing incidents occurring.

They are all super weary and stumbling around like inebriated cats. They know they must succeed with the Mars project or face a defeat in space.

The giant angle holes in the ground around the planet have been filled with nuclear explosives designed to serve as rocket propelled engines. The plan is to detonate the explosives in sequences and expel the planet like an incandescent twirler on a celebration day with momentum that moves the planet into an orbit position similar to that of Earth.

The control crew is comprised of a hundred people who are working at their designated areas on a strategically placed station for efficiency control.

No one is on the planet. Central control is regulated by electrodynamic magnetic and kinetic frequency modulation.

"All check points and stations ready for countdown," reads the operations director at a compuvision meter station.

The lead technician and his staff are initiating sensor instruments for countdown which regulates sequence propulsion.

Ten, nine, eight, seven, six, five, four, three, two, one—firing sequences are occurring methodically from the holes around the globe. The ground is beginning to rumble progressively louder with an ear splitting sound. Giant and fiery after burn smoke, steam and dirt spit and spue sporatically from the parameters of the holes as though the Lord of the universe was mad as the timing sequences modulate for control of direction.

Finally, the instrument measuring planet movement registers Mars as starting to move.

It is critical now, with the control station regulating the firing sequences, for the planet to move in the projected path fast enough, but not too fast so as to throw it out of control.

"Apply more thrust energy on sequence .00570 to compensate for .00578," A C.S. technician states. "Apply singular thrust control on vertical G.L. APEX. Initiate VAC stream coordinator seven degrees plus."

The control teams of scientists, engineers and technicians galore are racking their brains and sweating it out for an all out no return goal of moving this planet exactly where it has to go. They have no time to rub their noses or wipe the sweat off their brows. This is the point of no return! There is no margin for error. This could turn into an unprecedented and cataclysmic nightmare of which no humans ever experienced if it gets out of control.

The team is actually moving Mars off its orbital path as it moves forward on an angle toward the sun and Earth's orbit.

Are they really ready for this monstrous move? Well, it's too late for them to change their minds. It could be wonderful for or the end of a very confident, proud, assertive and creative species of living beings.

"Minus seven on TR sequence .00487. Plus six on TR sequence .00756. Two minutes until capacity load reduction," states the steering officer to the control panel crew minute by minute. "Minus ten on all sequences," he says.

"Minus fifteen on all sequences now!" he yells in a sweat.

The steering officer and control panel technicians are working almost frantically along with the other scientists and engineers who are logically trouble shooting orbital guidance control of the planet. The power of the sequence propulsion reactors have met their capacities to thrust and the planet is moving into the required distance from the sun which is now in a precise and direct path of Earth's orbit!

Earth's orbit is exactly where Tricoal intended it to be. What Tricoal hasn't anticipated is the tremendous propulsion thrust of Mars while heading toward Earth.

The control regulating crews work with a complex array of sensing devices designed to initiate and maintain the angle rotation and crow speed of the planet. They are manipulating sensors, pulling levers and shouting back and forth "reverse the sequence thrust." "Initiate emergency antithrust propulsion reactors."

The crews realize they must put on the brakes or Mars will travel at an inertia speed around the sun which exceeds that of planet Earth.

If they are unable to secure that braking, the inevitable conclusion will be a crash into Earth with an inconceivable concussion to say the least.

Tricoal's control panels consist of the most sophisticated equipment of mankinds time and the most brilliant and aggressive scientists the world of Earth has ever known. They have creative abilities that took many hundreds of years to develop.

These people of Tricoal are surely the chosen ones to lead in the search and promotion of mankind's destiny in the solar system. They surely wouldn't jeopardize or compromise the safety or survival of the species; would they?

"Energizing ATPR. Reverse sequence .00787, through .01798 to minus twenty on TH."

Everyone is exercising their own skill capacities to the maximum in a desperate attempt to slow the planet to even speed of Earth.

Earth's people have been doing a little developing of their own in recent years.

Since they have indulged themselves in self-chosen privileges on Earth, whether the survivors like it or not, the surviving Earth's people have also chosen a way to deal with them.

They have had meetings too. People around the world have been salvaging capsulecar remains and rebuilding them, along with the ones they confiscated, primarily for the use of traveling to world wide meetings as they have had in the past. The purpose of these meetings is for Earth people to arrive at decisions on, first, where they stand in relationship to the space station progress mongrels and second what should be done about the situation of defending themselves.

After pooling their world wide resources of ideas and finances for them, they arrived at a long term plan they can handle.

Number one is to build a better world wide communication system for the benefit of strengthening world community resources for health and defense.

Number two is to rebuild broken space observatories and add astrometric viewers to observe and study the type of progress occurring at the stations and Mars.

Time has passed and they have followed these rules with constant improvements and they are, at present, able to detect moving activity on and around Mars.

Their theory, on protection, is based on not trusting the station people. Actually, neither side trusts each other.

The survivors believe sooner or later by watching them closely, they may be able to avert, defend against or conquer the aggressive opponents.

They are discovering something unusual and interesting, at the moment, on their astrometric viewers.

The newly developed laserscopic measuring sensor, which assist the astrometric viewer for more accuracy, is detecting the movement of Mars.

"This is the craziest thing I've ever seen," said astrometric expert Joseph Mason to his house director. "We knew they were developing a team to exploit Mars, but we didn't know they were going to play ball with us! That planet is moving in a direct crows line toward us!"

"Quick," said Director Billings, "get our defense department on the com (what can a defense department possibly do when someone is throwing a planet at you?)."

The next few hours are filled with people communicating as never before. Again, from all practical appearances, time is running out.

One astronomer said, "We're on a path of total annihilation. We're all doomed to die!"

The defense department and people's representatives have gathered in a comparatively short period of time for an emergency meeting. Will the "experts" know what to do?

"If we're all doomed to die, let's give it one last shot," says demolition expert Greg Astenoff. Let's comprise a team of engineers and scientists to devise a plan for moving our planet over!"

"Remember the deal we made with Tricoal which was food for explosives? We did it on several occasions. We have quite a stockpile of nuclear explosives," he says.

These people aren't debating the subject in this type of emergency. They are accepting the most logical solution at the moment and saying go with it. So, the team is formed and the prognosis and cure are underway.

Many solutions are relative in engineering and scientific evaluation and this one is no exception.

The process to move the Earth enough to miss the oncoming planet is close to that of relocating Mars except on a much smaller technical scale.

The world's explosive arsenal is being moved to one side of the planet. They are arranged in such a way that when the timing is right for detonation, the world's largest explosions ever will happen with intentions of moving Earth—aside.

The team doesn't have the time for extensive engineering calculations and scientific preparation for controlling the speed of movement, so there is a huge risk when, by using the explosives to move the planet, it may move too far. Of course, the result would be extreme vulnerability in a new atmosphere and all would perish.

The alternative will be similar to playing pool with triggered hand grenades. Little or big, dying is dying.

The engineers and astrometric specialists are constantly evaluating when Mars will hit Earth with the possibility there may be some change. They only have one shot and they have to be absolutely correct with their calculations.

Back on the stations, the experts missed their calculations somewhat and Mars appears to have flown the coop.

The steering officer reiterates "more power on antithrust reactors." The operation manager bursts in madder than an old wet hen and says, "Why the hell aren't you using the magnetic reversion compensator to boost the antithrust vices?"

"You said never use it when momentum is to strong. You said it could overload the system and may shut everything down" the steering officer responded.

"Alright, sorry to yell at you. I'll take the responsibility and you help."

Together, with all the professional technology, they manage to activate the reverse angle propulsion and the planet is slowing down.

The real big problem now is controlled explosive energy is running very low. They have been using too much energy again, like on Earth, as though it was perpetual.

A quick communique to all Mars project workers is issued by the operations manager: "We have accomplished the great task of moving Mars in a general direction as planned. Calculations were off a little and the planet gained unanticipated speed of which has been ninety five percent controlled. Our explosive energy is almost gone and Mars is headed toward Earth. Mars is now in a position for a perfect climate, but the climate won't be any good when Mars hits Earth. It would be gambling if we used the remaining energy to bring Mars to a stop. It may not be complete. The logical solution would be to use that energy and move Mars closer to the sun a few thousand miles to pass safely by Earth," he says and continues:

"The temperature on Mars will be a little hotter than Earth being closer to the sun, but it's better to live on a hotter planet than it is to collide with Earth or move into the opposite position and freeze to death."

These experts aren't perfect, but they are the best known at this time.

It will take several months for Mars to be in a threatening proximity to Earth orbiting on it's present path.

The decision has been made. In the meantime, they are moving all the stations to the vicinity of Mars' present position for better control of moving the planet off the direct path of Earth.

While they are doing that, the people on Earth have no knowledge of this plan. They believe Mars is on a collision course with Earth and are preparing to blast the old world toward the sun very soon.

Efforts on Earth are underway in securing the explosives. They will be detonated in sequence of three blasts two seconds apart so the initial impact will have less shock effect on living beings.

The land area of the explosion is being cleared of humans and many animals.

The stations are slow moving, but they are moving faster than Mars in their pursuit to catch up with them.

Days are becoming weeks and both the Earth and station people are making preparations to fire their explosives not being aware of both sides preparing an act that will reset both planets on a collision course.

When that happens, both their supply of explosives will be exhausted and reversing the direction for either will be at an end.

Joseph Mason, the astrometric expert on Earth, says "Greg! Take a look at what I've discovered. Mars is frighteningly close and guess what else."

Greg Astonoff, the demolition expert, looks into the astrometric viewer and sees dots forming on one side of the moving planet.

"What are they," he inquired.

"Those are the stations moving on a direct path toward Mars! They must be up to something. I'll notify the defense chief."

A conference communique with several key people in the detonation department reveals suspicion, anger and fear of Tricoal boosting power behind Mars for a final destructive blow to Earth.

"Time is running short. I'll notify the chief detonation engineer. We need to commence detonation procedure to move Earth," says Charles Norton, recent department head elect. "We must stay one step ahead of them."

Aren't humans stupendous! They're always one step ahead. They've locked themselves into, what they believe, is a master plan to save the Earth, or is it to save their own hides. What kind of consciousness is luring this living protoplasm of space beings into blowing giant holes in the home bases that supports them?

Pick a planet. Earth? Mars? How about playing around with the moon. It would by easier to pick on. Just think, since they never seem to be satisfied and if they conducted similar activities on the Moon, they could create giant tidal waves that would give them plenty of water for showers and plenty of salt for their food. Too bad they would have to forfeit air in exchange. Oh well, such is the price of glory and satisfaction of progress.

People everywhere, in this day of time and space, have been so engrossed with their activities of surviving and sciences of progress, they have allowed their spiritual consciousness to dwindle.

That pertains to Tricoal's people too. If they don't get complete control of Mars, they won't have a planet to exploit or an earth to return to.

So, all the people everywhere are existing in a state of extreme fear and are beginning to look a little beyond their scavenging desperation of scientific progress programming. They are actually searching for which is perspective and eternal guidance, in their own ways of course, for strength and support.

Through the searching process of praying, meditating or whatever they are engaging in to raise their consciousness to a helpful level, they are generally becoming more relaxed for broadening their scope on what may be happening with humanity. After all, they are intelligent born beings; right?

This also includes the very strong, stable and objectively oriented Tricoal bunch who are, as well as Earth's survivors, asking questions as: "Maybe there is something beyond our perception that we missed. Let's look into it," which was speculated by astropsychologist Anna Beck.

Responses to that are, "We hadn't considered how Earth's people might be responding to our launching Mars," said Professor Kalenski. "We know they have visual capabilities that extend this far."

"What would we do, questions Anna Beck, if we were watching a planet moving toward us?"

"We would probably want to get out of the way," says Professor Kalenski.

"That sounds logical," she says.

"There's only one way they could do that," says Professor Kalenski, "with the explosives we exchanged for food and supplies. Wow! The question is, which way would they move?"

There's a lot of scuttlebutt in this super chess game where both sides can lose. After all the debate, is there problem solved?

"The situation is no longer a matter of just moving Mars into an appropriate position. It is a matter of all of us having a fifty, fifty chance of surviving a possible final life calamity. The major question is, which way is the best way for either one of us to move?"

The Tricoal echelon has gathered quite quickly in representing all the station people to take a vote. Emergency voting is allowed by the echelon.

"The vote is to slow Mars to a stop, move Mars toward the sun or move Mars away from the sun," says Mr. Maraste.

"Wait. I have an idea, interrupts a young lady technician walking over from a distant sensor machine. "Why don't we send someone to Earth and drop some fliers to hold up the ball game so we can talk about it. They may even have their communication system working."

"Great idea," says Professor Kalenski. "Add that to the voting and let's vote!"

Since there are not massive people to vote this time, the voting is accomplished quickly and most affirmatively by the Tricoal echelon.

They decided to go to Earth with the message.

A whipstreaker and crew are quickly on their way to Earth. The captain has ordered their propulsion at maximum crows speed. Asteroid threat is very little now and the odds of reaching Earth at this speed and path are largely in favor of the ship and crew.

The ship's energy launch is completed now and cruising through space at maximum speed passing asteroids as though they were winning a race.

Time has passed and Tricoal is, again, descending to a safe position above Earth.

Earth's survivors are still suspicious, but they have also been emotionally petrified and a little more humble for alternatives.

The ship's communication system is open and before the fliers are dropped, a proud voice appears on the com. "What is your mission this time, to take our valuables before you cream us?"

"We can understand your mistrust," said Captain Hastings, "but we have no time to discuss our differences. We're all at risk of being obliterated and we must make arrangements to prevent the worst possible calamity."

"How do we know it's not a manipulation?" asked the voice.

"It is definitely a manipulation to save us all," said the captain. "Everything is at stake now. To show you what I mean, we will take the risk of landing because if we don't, mankind's history will never be read again."

"We humbly request permission to land and prevent this oncoming disaster. What are you worried about? You know we're out numbered. Know this now! We were once all one. We can become one again!

The captain purposely descended to a most populated area so they would feel more powerful and less vulnerable and defensive.

The whipstreaker is hovering overhead like an old time helicopter waiting, waiting, waiting for an answer.

After hours of deliberation, the people of the recently formed security force on the ground cleared a landing spot and issued a demand to "land and submit yourselves unarmed as political prisoners pending the outcome of this encounter. If sincere intensions are justified, we may work together."

The landing procedure begins and this just may be the landing that starts another take off of mankind and their relentless efforts to excel; or at least survive.

The big "if" is standing out again, bigger than ever now. "If" all these people can remain rational and unselfish long enough to really care about saving these worlds for their unknown destiny, will they suffice to combine the fruits of their progress for preventing a disaster, for locating Mars to an agreeable position and for creating a new beginning for all those who have gained the profits of experience and knowledge?

The question remains, will all these efforts to combine for mutual satisfaction lead to solving the problem that existed before and during the time Arthur Flintstock crusaded for population control?

Stretching the imagination a little may conclude a conceivable possibility mankind will continue to maintain progress in constant space development even at the cost of eternal suffering.

The final paradoxical conclusion may be anguish and insecurity of pain is what supplies the drive to expand. Time will tell.

The people of your time have the opportunity to influence natural destiny by taking heed to the possibilities mentioned in this terrifying and adventurous tale.

If you do, you must not wait too long lest you be caught in a vacuum of unpreventable and possibly unconquerable dilemmas.

I leave you now to transform into my future time. I may appear at your doorstep at another phase of space time continuum when further perception of understanding seems necessary for dealing with the unfolding or paradox of planet Earth's progress. You're friend D.B. 1438-GR0008.

The next issue of "Paradox Of Progress #2" is a continued and exciting story of change in the distant future of mankind in their ambitious, fearful and ideosyncratical nature of which causes unexpected surprises in that future.

It's another mind stretching experience of which growing mankind will need to stretch with in their paradoxical progress as time passes. See how the people you have grown to know in the book, pick up the pieces and move on into the next issue.

Your author, Lloyd E. McIlveen unveils a chronological list of many and various book subjects presenting controversial, educational, uplifting, futuristic, self-helping, philosophical, psychological, entertaining and other stimulating concepts of which are and will be displayed with brief descriptions of each book as follows:

1. "Evaluating Outdated Beliefs" This is a report, viewed through the perception of your author of the evolutionary process and changes occurring in belief; especially in the area of religion and spirituality. This was designed for the benefit of broadening individual perception, perspective and viewing "another" plane of belief while revealing fallacies in theological indoctrination. This is an improved revision of the book's origin.

2. "Staying Alive On Planet Earth I" This is a psychology of health required to stabilize and

maintain better health for the benefit of living a much longer life. Source: A lifetime of study, problems, recoveries and many successes more in natural methods.

3. "Understanding Loss To Relieve The Anguish" Loss of anything involves many distractions and disrupting emotional disarray. Gaining greater understanding of these emotions offsets the misery of them and enhances optimism of confidence and support for emotional weakness before, at and during the time of loss.

4. "Understanding Preventing And Eliminating Cancer" presents new views on the wonders of natural methods for practical use.

5. "Paradox Of Progress Unfolding I" This is a tale told by a man "many" centuries into the future about an exciting, overwhelming and terrifying occurrence on planet Earth as a result of their wondrous progress around the

time of 2300 A.D. Hang onto your seats! #2 is a second issue later on the list.

6. "Offsetting Climate Change And Nuclear Waste Contamination" This view of the two exposes the hazards, inevitabilities and possible solutions needed now for preventing a "too late" disaster that will affect all living beings too soon.

7. "What God Is And Is Not" This is a study of spiritual possibilities designed, not particularly to remold conventional mannerisms of belief, but to open and expand perception in the most controversial subject of mankind; the subject of God and whether mankind will or won't expand that consciousness along with all progress and growth on Earth and in the universe.

8. "Kids Of The Crick" This is a story of four old fashioned country kids setting out on a

weekend adventure in their countryside of tall grass, mountains, rivers, animals, caves and strange living beings. Sometimes, they aren't sure whether it's all real or not.

9. "Paradox Of Destiny Explained" eliminates the mysteries, facades, fantasies and deceptions of how, where, way and when we do what we do and opens new possibilities for expanding, our beliefs and consciousness pertaining to this study of available options that may influence insight for growth, change or even justify present mannerisms of what may control the individual, planet Earth or the whole universe and is not zealous, fanatic or bigoted; only assertively revealing.

10. "Paradox Of Progress Unfolding 2" This book is a continued fiction story and can be considered exemplary of "major" human changes that alienated millions of people to another planet in the future. They are led by

the elements of unexpected surprises of which is par for the course with gutsy space pioneers. The first "Paradox Of Progress Unfolding I" must be read first to understand and appreciate the disproportional attitudes and positions of people on a threshold of major change and disasters upon them. This is not only a tale of travel, trials and tribulations, it is philosophically stimulating and adds toward future insightful expansion of the human species.

11. "Staying Alive On Planet Earth 2" This is all extended version of the original psychology of health for living a longer life. More knowledge allows more life.

12. "Preventing The Doom Of Mankind" This is a stimulating, vitalizing and somewhat shocking description of how mankind is "truly" faced with extinction in the "near" future due to their own faults of progress. It's very educational

and needed now to help offset that inevitability where the odds dictate we will all perish if we don't adhere to this offsetting of which "is" possible to achieve.

13. "Spiritual Transformation Of The Fourth Millennium" Old-time conventional religion is fading. New-time spirituality is on the rise. Objective realism is the prime issue here for future inclined thinking and believing.

14. "Understanding The Science Of Creative Mind" This is a study for discovering, developing and practicing a psychological powerhouse within for conquering the unconquerable, achieving the impossible or doing things no one has done all depending on, of course, the makeup and determination of the individual. This study brings out a greater potential of the individual's abilities when taken seriously. This was compiled from

a lifetime of study and experience from your author.

15. "Living to 150" is a guidance program for intentions of anyone desiring a longer than longer life which is insightfully and innovatively educational for that purpose.

16. "The Act Of Getting One's Act Together" If anyone, business or nation wants to develop their stance, priorities and position in life, this is a chance for them to get their act together more than ever.

17. "Making Changes From This Point Forward" The design of this book is for the purpose of preventing repeated mistakes of unforeseen surprises due to what we weren't or aren't aware of that did, can or will happen again. It's all about gaining or rearranging change consciousness in this area.

18. "Relationships For All" This is a carefully arranged view of how relationships can

function much better when initiated or guided by the experiences of many experts and your author who have had failures and successes in their very human encounters. The experiences of more relationships result in wiser judgments and approaches to others.

19. "The We Between Us" helps us in discovering who is good for us and who is not. First it is a study in the book. Then it is a study with people of what exists in two party's minds (individuals business or nations) when first confronted. A real time saver in evaluating possible compatibility or not between the two for anyone. It works.

20. "Passion Of Dance" This is a narrative on progress, value and guidance for the dance inclined. It's informative and inspiring with its history and recent magnetism.

21. "Open That Door" to love. This book is comprehensively all about love. It's not a

storybook. It clears up the differences of love that causes misunderstanding, suspicion and deception.

22. "Get The Spirit" This book describes controversial and somewhat intertwined conventional views of spirit, spirits and spirituality. This book untangles the "usual" views and presents a more perspective manner of living with these concepts of mind.

23. "Stories Of What They Couldn't Or Wouldn't Tell" Ages are from babies to 100 years; twenty four of them.

24. "Improving On Love And Relationships" This one is two books in one. Part one "Open That Door" is a psychology of love that enhances perspective to understand and adapt to a very popular, but deceiving, repressed and ignored emotion; love. Part two covers "Relationships For All" which elaborates on origination, different types,

significance, deceptions, desires, experiences, communication, possibilities, future and guidance of relationships. It's comprehensive and also derived from a lifetime of relationship experiences and serious study.

NOTES

NOTES

NOTES

NOTES

NOTES

www.ingramcontent.com/pod-product-compliance
Lightning Source LLC
Chambersburg PA
CBHW030435290526
45786CB00001B/303